They Found Our Engineer

The Story of Arthur Goddard.
The Land Rover's first Engineer.

Michael Bishop

authorHOUSE®

AuthorHouse™ UK Ltd.
500 Avebury Boulevard
Central Milton Keynes, MK9 2BE
www.authorhouse.co.uk
Phone: 08001974150

© 2011 Michael Bishop. All rights reserved.

No part of this book may be reproduced, stored in a retrieval system, or transmitted by any means without the written permission of the author.

First published by AuthorHouse   05/02/2011

ISBN: 978-1-4567-7758-6 (sc)

Any people depicted in stock imagery provided by Thinkstock are models, and such images are being used for illustrative purposes only. Certain stock imagery © Thinkstock.

Because of the dynamic nature of the Internet, any web addresses or links contained in this book may have changed since publication and may no longer be valid. The views expressed in this work are solely those of the author and do not necessarily reflect the views of the publisher, and the publisher hereby disclaims any responsibility for them.

Special thanks.

Special thanks to Spen King, Geof Miller and Roger Crathorne, who all worked together on the original Range Rover project at Rover in the 1960s. Without their help, this book would not have been possible. Roger's input was incredible. The archive material that he and Land Rover supplied added immensely to the great story that Arthur shares with us all. Also, thanks to the Land Rover Register 1948 to 1953 and the Land Rover Series 1 clubs for their help as well. A very special thanks as well to Chris King and Penny Walker.

Land Rover enthusiasts across the world from Lode Lane, Solihull to Sydney, Australia were stunned when they heard of Arthur's story. Like me, Land Rover fanatics had read all the books and magazines and spent years wondering how it all happened. I had done extensive research on the very early vehicles and could not believe what I was hearing from Arthur sixty years after production had begun. It is a pleasure to be able to share Arthur's story about the early days of Land Rover's development.

Contents

Introduction: History floats to the surface	ix
The Land Rover.	1
Arthur's Story	5
The start of the 'Special Project'	8
A huge hit before Amsterdam.	13
Assistant Chief Engineer	16
Setting out the Land Rover's DNA, 1949 to 1957	18
How do you find someone that you do not know is missing?	26
The Boy from the Outback	32
Mountains of Information	37
The Final Pieces of the Jigsaw.	41
The Patience of Youth	43
Are you sure?	46
What we did find!!!	52
The Factory Plans	67
The Ash Cloud nerves	73
An Evening with Arthur Goddard	82
The follow up	89
An Afternoon Chat with Spen and Arthur	97
The post Rover years onwards	126
Arthur disappears to Sydney.	130
The post retirement Career	134

Introduction: History floats to the surface

At the Land Rover 50th anniversary in 1998, little was known of Arthur's story. Ten years later at the 60th anniversary in 2008, the situation was much the same. Even though many parts of the early Land Rover story were already known, it was not clear how the full story fitted together. The parts of the known story included:
- "the stop gap"
- the Centre Steer prototype
- the run away success of the Land Rover and
- the rapid pace of development from the original appearance of the Pre Production number 01 in March 1948 to full mass production by December at the end of 1948.

To call it a case of 'corporate amnesia' would be a touch harsh. Jaguar Land Rover and its' various keepers since the Land Rover began are in the business of developing and selling new and often very high specification vehicles. It is a very complicated and competitive industry that includes managing everything to do with factories, employees, unions, and suppliers, amongst others.

Once the work for last year's model is completed, car companies focus on the next year's design. With vehicle production, a mountain of work goes into a new design. Journalists provide some insight into the scale of this mountain when a new model is released. Corporate memory fades as staff change jobs and people leave the company. In their enthusiasm to learn more about the vehicles, enthusiasts and collectors rediscover the lost history by gradually collecting nuggets about engineering changes and vehicle developments. Thankfully Rover had documented a broad picture of what was done but the full story still needed to be uncovered. The way the early Land Rover story was told simply didn't make sense to many closely interested in it. The story that had been told was Maurice Wilks had an old wartime Jeep that he found particularly useful for light work around his properties. His brother Spencer Wilks, Rover's managing director asked "What would Maurice do when he needed to replace the Jeep?" The realisation came that there wasn't really an option, and Maurice thought Rover could make a similar vehicle. It was to be just a post war stop gap for Rover. This enabled Rover to produce a vehicle that would sell to farmers and industry for a few years while they waited for the return of their traditional luxury car market. The Land Rover was a huge success after its' introduction at the 1948 Amsterdam Motor show and became the Rover Company's top selling vehicle. The only problem with this simplified story is evidence of a huge development in the early Land Rover 80" vehicles. Why would anyone risk spending so much time, resources and money on developing a 'stop gap' vehicle to sell for just a few years? In addition, in the immediate post war years, Britain didn't have money to waste.

The original Centre Steer Prototype in November 1947

There just were not any answers for many of the simple questions about the first Land Rovers. These questions started with the basic, yet intriguing, Centre Steer prototype. Using a Jeep rolling chassis and a Rover engine, Maurice Wilks designed and assembled the Centre Steer prototype. Many photos of this vehicle still exist with it ploughing, towing trailers and fording streams. But what happened to it? Shortly after the Centre Steer disappeared in 1948, the conventional Land Rover appeared with right and left hand drive steering, doors, windows and a full canvas hood. Not long after the Land Rover's introduction, factory winches and the hard top option and other developments were added on. Very much the Land Rover we know and love. People, however; would ask questions such as, "Wasn't it supposed to have Central Steering?" and "Was it just a stop gap?"

There was very little knowledge about how the model range evolved into what we still know and appreciate today with multiple wheelbases and body styles. That was until Arthur reappeared in 2009.

The Land Rover.

The Land Rover is a vehicle that is instantly recognisable anywhere, either as any one of the Series 1, 2 of 3 range or today's Defender models. It is an iconic vehicle known and loved worldwide after more than 60 years in production and sales almost everywhere. After the first 30 or so years in production, the Land Rover became a brand itself. In the modern world, it is a huge international British automotive brand, which happens to have another iconic vehicle within its stable, The Range Rover. The more recent models, the Discovery and the Freelander, are part the "Land Rover Legend" and have been added to again with the Range Rover Sport and the Range Rover Evoque. From the true die hard enthusiasts' point of view, there is still the ghost of a third marque in the once great Rover Company Limited, which in its' hey day was advertised as 'One of Britain's Fine Cars.'

Visitors today to the Land Rover factory at Lode Lane, Solihull, enjoy the home of the 'Land Rover Experience' for all that its worth. Off road rides are available in Land Rover's new and historic vehicles. These are driven over the jungle test track, up hills and through vast puddles. Promotional goodies like polo shirts, toys, dvds and umbrellas are available to purchase after the ride. Almost a stone's throw away, Land Rover Defenders are assembled in much the same way as they have been since 1948. The combination of friendly staff, production lines and the Land Rover marques, mean that the heart of the old Rover Company is still very much in place.

Michael Bishop

The 2011 model Land Rover Defender

Members of staff still happily speak about the days of the great 1960s cars, the Rover P6s and Rover P5B V8 coupes. Often they talk about the old Rover cars in context to today's new models being shown. Starting as apprentices in the 1960s, they worked in each area to understand what the company did and how it operated. Through this they developed an understanding of the breadth and depth of what Rover did in all the different departments that came to produce motor vehicles. All this knowledge came from the fine engineering experience that has been built up in the firm since at least 1885. Certainly, when the first production Land Rovers left Solihull in 1948, this was from a company that had been producing cars already for 44 years and had sold tens of thousands of them. When the Land Rover was born, Rover certainly did know what it was doing.

In more recent times, the Rover brand split from the Land Rover side. The modern day Jaguar Land Rover firm was formed following a chaotic time brought about by company sales, mergers and splits leading on from the late 1960s. But that is another story. The recent homecoming of the Rover name brought a touch of harmony back to the history of Land Rover that today is going from strength to strength.

The Rover Company finds its original roots in the 19th century with J K Starley and Co. and Starley's invention of the Rover safety bicycle, the basis of modern pedal power bicycle. As with many of these great innovative Victorian companies, one engineering marvel led to another. In the period leading up to the First World War, Rover cars and motorcycles were a popular and very respected make. J K Starley died in 1901, just before the production of the first real Rover car. The post First World War period of the 1920s and 30s was a rocky time for many manufacturers. Rover survived by the skin of its teeth. Its survival was due to strength of its core business and the depth of its engineering expertise.

The foundations of the current Land Rover side to Jaguar Land Rover began when Spencer Wilks joined Rover in 1930 as the Board of Directors were looking for someone to really lead the company forward. Wilks had studied law and had worked at Hillman. With Rover, Wilks now had the chance to manage his 'own' company and the Wilks name became synonymous with Rover for decades to come. Like many others, Rover experienced significant financial turmoil as a consequence of the 1929 stock market crash. Spencer Wilks brought good and trusted people to Rover, including his younger brother, Maurice who was head of the technical side of the Company.

After the Wilks brother took over, Rovers cars became very highly respected in the 1930's. They provided very good quality motoring. Bank managers, doctors, and professional people bought Rovers. By the end of the 1930s, the order books were full. With the onset of the Second World War, Rover was heavily involved in the war effort on many different fronts. Rover produced various wartime machinery, including planes and tank engines and was involved in specialist engineering projects such as the jet engine development with Frank Whittle. Rover's war time projects resulted in company becoming a large operation with multiple factories. By then, Rover, a solid and respected manufacturer, had more than 55 years engineering experience. In that time, Rover had designed and manufactured bicycles, cars and motorcycles. Engine gearboxes, differentials and chassis frames were core components that Rover manufactured. Most parts were made in-house and always had been.

For the young apprentice engineer in the 1930s and 40s pre war and wartime era, Rover Company Limited was ideal. It was a great place to get a foot in the door and to get your career started, which is very much the same today at Jaguar Land Rover. Rover's modern day growth started in the mid 1930s. In the 1930s, Rover was involved with the shadow factory scheme to meet Britain's wartime needs, initially for manufacturing aircraft with the onset of World War II. Rover grew steadily, and in the 1960s was taken over by British Leyland. Rover's success was founded on

Michael Bishop

the Wilks brothers' ability to run Rover, make cars with great appeal and to spot and develop talent in their employees. In the years being taken over by British Leyland, the company has been owned by British Aerospace, BMW, Ford and Tata.

Arthur and I taking a look at Dave Hanson's 1949 80" Land Rover

Arthur's Story

Like most lives, Arthur Goddard's started off on a simple straight path. He was born in January 1921, the second son of John Newman Goddard and Ruth, who was always known as Tuttie. Arthur's father was a professional soldier. Arthur was born in Belfast where his father was stationed at the time. The family moved to Bromborough in Merseyside. Arthur attended the Little Sutton Church of England School in Bromborough and after finishing school, he completed a mechanical engineering certificate at a college in Liverpool. With this qualification, he joined the war effort, testing World War II aero engines for problems operating at high altitudes. Arthur enjoyed his job and continued in this field of work. He moved to Coventry and worked at Alvis in the Aero Engine research laboratory, where they tested various wartime airplane engines made by allies, foes and neutral countries alike.

Towards the end of the war, the Department of Labour was preparing for demobilisation and the return of servicemen and women who would be in need of jobs and homes. Many of the UK based wartime related jobs were reassessed; and Arthur's position was no different. He hoped to stay within the aero engine test facility, but when the Department of Labour found out he had experience in the Rolls Royce Merlin Aircraft Engine, they sent him to Rover for an interview with Technical Head, Maurice Wilks. Rover had a problem. Rover's head of engines, Jack Swaine, had broken both his legs in a motorcycle accident and was off recuperating. Rover needed desperately a replacement engineer with Merlin engine experience to take over at the Acock's Green factory. Rover was adapting this engine for use in tanks; and Arthur got the job filling in for Jack.

Arthur did not want to leave the Aero Engine research laboratory, but he had no choice in the matter.

Rover and Arthur Goddard became a good team. Once the war had ended in Europe in 1945, Maurice Wilks was eager to get back in the car game. He moved Arthur, who was in his early 20s, from the Meteor project and put him onto Rover car engines, to develop a tensioner for Rover's new 4 and 6 cylinder 'inlet over exhaust' engines. These engines were still in development and had a lot of rattle in the timing chain area that was related to torsional vibration of the camshaft.

Arthur suddenly found the work a lot more interesting. As he was not a pilot, he could never fly the aero engines he worked on, but a car engine was a different thing. With cars, Arthur could do all the theory and testing and then enjoy the experience of driving the vehicle himself. After six months convalescence, Jack Swaine returned to work and stepped back into control of the engine area. By then, Arthur had fixed the timing chain by making a sprung tensioner with a pulley wheel arrangement.

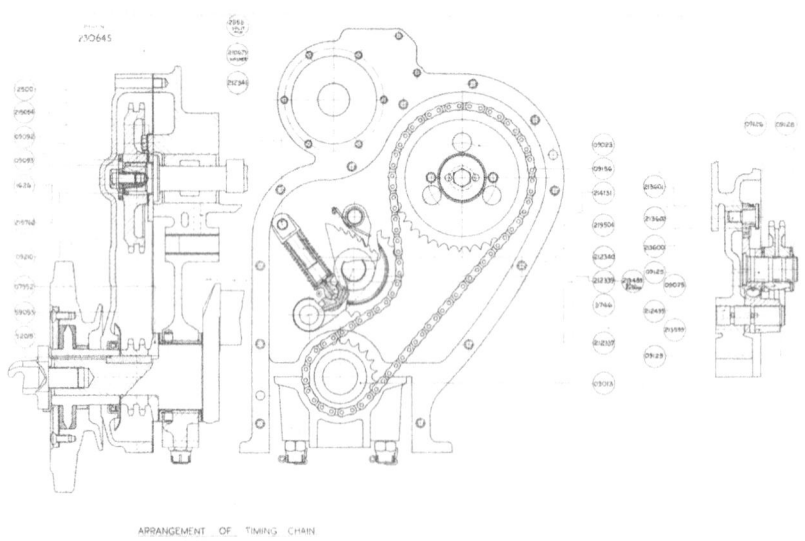

The timing chain and tensioner of the Rover 'Inlet Over Exhaust Engine'

Arthur had been testing the engines in the research laboratory and stayed on there. In the research laboratory, he worked for Dizzy Drew. After Dizzy's departure to Rolls Royce, Arthur became the research laboratory head. He was starting to build a reputation for being able to get things done. Not long after landing the research laboratory job, the development engineer, Rosy, left in unexplained circumstances. After Rosy's departure, Arthur became the development engineer as well, focussing on car noise and vibration, including Rover's unreleased post war small M type car. Most of the people working for Maurice Wilks were specialists:- engine people, design people, gear box, suspension, all specialists in the many areas of automotive engineering. The specialist engineers were limited to there own areas. The development engineer, dealt with the complete vehicles, and the chief engineer Robert Boyle was the other broad based engineer there under Technical Director, Maurice Wilks. A specialist would lead small projects and the broad projects were given to Arthur. Being in control of the research laboratory had its uses. People often needed favours done quickly. Arthur, true to his reputation of getting things done, was able to do those favours. And he would get his favours repaid when he was in need of help and resources.

After Arthur had been at Rover for three years, Maurice Wilks presented the idea of the Land Rover in an engineering meeting. Arthur felt that the beauty of these engineering meetings was that they were very informal and often called at short notice. At the meetings were chief engineer Robert Boyle and production engineer Olaf Poppe, head of the drawing office George Seale, chassis engineer Gordon Bashford, gearbox specialist Frank Shaw and head engine man Jack Swaine.

In the meetings, there was much discussion about development projects, and what plans were in the pipeline. If something needed to be followed up in the next few days, then the jointly held view was that "maybe we'll get together tomorrow sometime in the afternoon and have another look at this bit." Meetings could be called at a minute's notice if something needed immediate attention. Flexibility of decision making was, in Arthur's opinion, one of the reasons for Rover's success. Arthur believes that with engineering, the answer to something is almost always already known. But implementation often loses its way in the bureaucracy of having to go to this committee and that committee and get approval from here, and go to accounts and get the budget and alter the budget, etc. In the days when the Wilks managed Rover, engineers would just get together and say "we want to do this and this and this" and they would all say "yes, yes, yes" or "no, no, no." As a consequence, engineering decisions were made quickly and engineering projects implemented without delay.

The start of the 'Special Project'

Arthur felt that from the start the Land Rover project was perceived as special. The idea arose from Maurice Wilks' experience with his Wartime Jeep and its usefulness at light farming and small jobs. In 1947, Wilks swapped a Bren Gun carrier for his Kenilworth neighbour, Colonel Nash's 'well used' Jeep. Maurice found the Jeep effective at clearing snow during the hard winter of 1947. He had the Jeep registered for road use in 1947 and found it just as great around the Wilks' beachside property on Anglesey, the birthplace of the idea to build Land Rovers.

Early testing of Land Rover number 1 *Huey*.
Johnny Cullen driving, Arthur passenger

Immediately after WWII, the British economy was in dire need of foreign currency. Through rationing of steel for home market use, the British government encouraged British car companies to increase foreign exports and discouraged the use of steel for the manufacture of cars for the home market. The Land Rover had huge export potential for Rover. Seizing the opportunity, Maurice Wilks continued working on his idea by modifying an ex Army Jeep. The Jeep was changed to have a Rover 1.6 litre engine and aluminium bodywork with central steering like a tractor. This became the 'Centre Steer' prototype Land Rover. The vehicle was made in September 1947. The original idea was for the Land Rover to be a low volume stop gap vehicle to keep the company ticking along, producing 50 vehicles per week. The design team did not have much off road driving experience and had very little farming experience. Arthur and the other engineers were not impressed with many aspects of the Centre Steer vehicle and felt they could do much more with it. The main issues they had with the Centre Steer were that it was awkward to drive and in some instances dangerous. The main problem was that sitting in the middle of the vehicle negatively impacted the driver's ability see oncoming traffic around a vehicle ahead. In addition, the gear lever was very awkward to operate.

As development engineer, Arthur became the leader and co-ordinator of the Land Rover project. His team included the other specialist engineers. They quickly started the work of designing the Land Rover. One initial task was to inform major suppliers of Rover's requirements and get their commitment to be ready to supply. Another task was to get a thorough understanding of existing four wheel drive vehicles. The team purchased a few Jeeps and took them apart piece by piece to develop a full understanding about how they worked. Arthur recalls that the Wilks brothers, Spencer and Maurice, and chief engineer Robert Boyle discussed in great detail what the Land Rover should and should not include.

Once the vehicle design was agreed, Arthur and the rest of the engineers were fully committed to doing what was needed to put the Land Rover into production. At this early point in the project, Arthur remembers that all were happy with the production target of 50 vehicles per week. Arthur's priorities were to oversee the project to manufacture the off road vehicle and to appreciate the needs of the agricultural market, specifically farmers' requirements for ploughing and for power take off work.

After Standard of Coventry installed the Standard car engine in the Ferguson Tractor, Arthur looked closely at how the power and torque characteristics of that engine were adapted for agricultural use. For the 1948 model year, Rover introduced the 1.6 litre 4 cylinder inlet over exhaust engine range to the new Rover P3 Rover '60' car. From the beginning, this was also the planned engine for the Land Rover.

Arthur mentioned they had a very careful look at how the Jeep was made and how well it had survived in service during the war. Considering what they were trying to make, they would have been crazy if they had not made a close study of it. Using the Jeep as a basis, the Land Rover team made many parts that little bit bigger and stronger than the Jeep's, including the gears. By Christmas 1947, the full design of the Land Rover was set out on an 80" wheelbase. Unlike the Jeeps steel body it used aluminium bodywork made from a new alloy called Birmabright. The Rover engineers had identified that corrosion was a serious issue with Jeeps and that aluminium could be used to limit corrosion.

The people that Arthur worked with came up with the brilliant simplicity that has endeared so many to the Land Rover for generations. It was very much a team effort from Arthur's point of view. Gordon Bashford designed the main chassis frame. Olaf Poppe designed the box sectioning of the chassis and the simplicity of the body work, which was designed with as little presswork as possible. Arthur praises Olaf as a production wizard. The box section chassis was a new design at the time and a brilliant piece of engineering. Poppe did a brilliant job in working out how to make it. Frank Shaw created the transfer box. The engineers incorporated the Rover freewheel unit in the drive train for the front axle of the Land Rover. The freewheel unit has a function similar to a bicycle freewheel to help with fuel economy of the car. For the Land Rover, the freewheel allows the front wheels to turn faster than the rear when going around corners, enabling permanent four wheel drive. And Jack Swaine, Rover's engine designer was kept up with the requirements for the engine that resulted in slightly lowering the compression for the Land Rover.

They Found Our Engineer

Goddard and Cullen again in *Huey* testing off road

The Land Rover, as we know it, came to life in the first two '48 Pre Production vehicles, numbers 01 and 02 in mid March 1948. In the development phase for the Land Rover, Arthur had Johnny Cullen take on all the driving and testing duties. Arthur's other right hand man was Ralf Nash who worked in the engineering department on the development vehicles. The first test was to make sure that the clearances for all the moving items in the drive train were as designed and that nothing scraped, knocked or moved irregularly. Holes were cut into the bodywork of the first Pre Production prototype to be able to see what was happening.

A problem arose with the front differential seizing. The Rover car differential was fitted to the Land Rover rear and front axles to provide four wheel drive. This differential was not designed to operate on the front axle and to turn in the opposite direction at speed. The result was that the rotation of the differential on the front axle forced the oil away from the centre of the differential causing the front differential to seize.

Aside from these two problems, the Land Rover was ready for more general testing. The Land Rovers were tested through a large ford on the local river Blythe and also on the beach at Anglesey in Wales near Maurice Wilks' holiday home. Arthur knew that potential Land Rover customers required diesel engines because the petrol engine electrics suffered from getting wet during the deep fording test. Land Rover could not immediately supply diesel engines, but were keen to do so.

The remaining Pre Production vehicles were used to refine the original design. Subsequent Pre Production vehicles were used for many different development uses, from sales and marketing to agricultural and military testing. Arthur received Pre Production vehicle number 36, which was used for agricultural testing. At Arthur's request, a test track for the vehicles within the factory grounds was constructed. The test track went over the top of air raid shelters and through Billsmore Wood that adjoins the Solihull Works, and is part of the Land Rover Experience centre today. A vehicle of the Land Rover's type, with an alloy based body, had never been manufactured before. As a result, the engineers had quite a lot to learn and needed to learn it fast.

In the midst of the Land Rover development, Arthur had other projects he was working on too. The Rover P4 car development was in full swing with various items needing testing and further development. In addition, the Rover gas turbine engine was about to be fitted into a car chassis for testing. For the Rover gas turbines, Arthur had designed a balancing machine for the compressor blades with a spin high revolution of around 40,000. Arthur later became involved with the testing and running of Jet 1, Rover's first gas turbine car, with Spencer and Maurice Wilks' nephew, Spen King.

A huge hit before Amsterdam.

The 'official' Birthday of the Land Rover is the 30th of April 1948. It was the day the Land Rover made its debut at the 1948 Amsterdam Motor show. It was a Friday and one of the first motor shows after the war. In development terms, this was still very early days for the Land Rover with less than 10 of the Pre Production vehicles ready. Arthur and his colleague, Johnny Cullen, delivered two Land Rovers to Amsterdam for the show. This was Arthur's first trip abroad. One of the vehicles, the Pre Production vehicle number 05 was a Mobile Welding development vehicle with a Lincoln SA 150 belt drive welding unit fitted between the driver and passenger seats and driven from the centre power take off.

The Land Rover at the 1948 Amsterdam Motor Show.

Arthur did not have too much to do with the sales and marketing side of the company. To help promote such a new and still in development vehicle, Arthur and Johnny Cullen manned the Rover stand to answer technical questions that the sales team had not been briefed about. Also on the stand was Bob Swann, the chief engineer at Lincoln Electric, who had supplied the welding units for the vehicles and the welding machines that welded together the main chassis rails of the Land Rover.

The show was a great success. Arthur recalls that the Land Rover was very well received at the show, with people interested in both agricultural and military uses. One vehicle was in the main hall and another outside for demonstration use. Arthur and the team were already feeling very confident about the Land Rover's future. The word had been steadily spreading through the motor industry of a 'Jeep-like' vehicle being developed by one of the big Midland's based car firms. The British military had been in contact very early on and were already very keen on purchasing up to 1000 vehicles. The military were Land Rover's main market and development work on the farming side would be a second priority. So far, the investment cost of getting the vehicle to this point had been small. Nonetheless, the idea of the Land Rover being a small production stop gap had long gone with the Centre Steer.

Now officially announced, in May 1948 the Land Rover was shown at many of the major British agricultural shows. News from the Amsterdam Motor Show was also spreading quickly worldwide. During May and June 1948, more development items were ironed out and the specification set for the first production Land Rovers. The first production models rolled off the make shift production line in July 1948. From idea to production the Land Rover time line was roughly 10 months. To this day, this must be one of the fastest mass produced vehicles to go from concept to prototype through development and into production in Britain. The Ministry of Supply received their first two Pre Production vehicles numbers 29 and 30 for extensive testing. As the news of the new vehicle spread, orders from all over the Commonwealth, as well as many other parts of the world, had amassed in an incredibly short time. As the Land Rover was a commercial vehicle, it did not incur a British sales tax. Rover was very pleased with this outcome; and being sales tax free was often clearly stated in Land Rover advertisements.

The Land Rover was an enormous success. On 21 July 1948, a week before King George VI received his first vehicle, Rover managing director, Spencer Wilks announced to the Rover board that

'the extensive enquiries for the Land Rover from Home and abroad amounted to approximately 8000 vehicles and that in the face of such potential demand that production be expanded to 500 vehicles per week and that also a view to reducing production costs so that Rover could be in a position to meet competition.'

The demand for the Land Rover was exceptional. To meet demand and stay ahead of competition, Rover faced the challenge of a dramatic increase in production (remember it was 50 in the pre production phase) and reducing production costs. The Land Rover was transformed from a "stop gap" project to a full production model. The stage was well set for a huge development program with Arthur Goddard as one of the instrumental leaders.

Assistant Chief Engineer

One of Arthur's first Land Rover production projects was, in fact, to build the proper production line for the Land Rover, designed to run at 18" per minute. It was around this time that Arthur was appointed Assistant Chief Engineer. Once the production line was in place and fully operational at the end of August/start of September, Arthur started to look at the next stage of development. They were well aware by this point that one of the limitations of the 80" wheelbase was in the load space in the rear. Trailers were the obvious and simple answer. First was the development of the Brockhouse Land Rover trailer that became an option for increased carrying capacity. They had tested all sorts of agricultural attachments with the Land Rover as well at this stage too. In late October 1948 the first vehicle was dispatched to the Motor Industry Research Association (MIRA). The Land Rover at MIRA was the first vehicle there on a permanent basis at the test facility. Jaguar Land Rover continues to use MIRA's test facilities to this day.

After the war, MIRA was designated as a facility for the export testing of British vehicles. Its objective was to replicate conditions in many of the far away destinations that British cars found themselves in. The MIRA test facility is still going strong. It was originally built as a joint venture by the post war motor industry. Each of the manufacturers involved in MIRA after the war had their own area to add to the facility, to help with Britain's export drive. Rover part was the Belgian Pavé facility.

The real Pavé in Belgium destroyed a car's suspension in as little as 6 months. Replicating Pavé conditions for testing purposes would be a great test to prove the new 'export quality' demands for British manufactured vehicles. It was also perfect for the Land Rover that was heading very

They Found Our Engineer

quickly to some very inhospitable roads in unknown corners of the globe. Arthur recalled that he and Bro Ward visited and studied a particularly nasty section of the Pavé near the start of the, then new, Jabeck Highway in Belgium. After carefully measuring and mapping the surface of the Pavé, they returned to MIRA and found similar stones which they used to perfectly replicated Rover's own mile long section of Pavé.

An early 1948 Land Rover on the Belgian Pavé at MIRA

This kind of testing was all new to the Land Rover engineers. The first step was to decide what was a reasonable test. The engineers set a standard that all Rover vehicles had to be able to do 1000 miles on the Pavé. One thousand driven miles on the Pavé put immense stress throughout the whole vehicle and bodywork and anything that was not strong enough broke. The Pavé testing of shock absorbers was quite difficult and engineering compromises had to be made. Finding a shock absorber that would do a 1000 miles on the Pavé was not necessarily the right one for the Land Rover. A shock absorber that did not break may not have worked hard enough to sufficiently control the vehicle. One that lasted 800 miles may have been the best compromise to ride, where one that lasted only 300 miles certainly was not good enough.

Production in November 1948 had reached over 100 vehicles per week and was growing. In December, to speed up production the pressed main bulkhead replaced the hand made version. By the end of February 1949 the first Completely Knocked Down Land Rover (known as CKD) sailed to Regent Motors of Melbourne for local assembly in Australia.

Setting out the Land Rover's DNA, 1949 to 1957

Heading into 1949 with a filled a order book from across the world, Arthur and his team set on a path that led to the full establishment of the Land Rover as a model range in its' own right. The list of development vehicles sent to Arthur and the Development Department was numerous to say the least. The Ministry of Defence (MOD) had shown a huge amount of interest in the Land Rover. An initial batch of twenty 1948 models was followed up with a large order of nearly two thousand Land Rovers to be delivered towards the end of 1949 and the start of 1950. The MOD proposed improvements for the Land Rover and sent these directly to Arthur. Customers and employees, alike, provided input to further improve and develop the Land Rover. The MOD continued to be Rover's main customer. In fact, The MOD had been Rover's main customer since showing interest in the early the development days before the 1948 Amsterdam show.

They Found Our Engineer

A brand new Land Rover Defender on the factory floor

One of the first production developments was a very early trial of the two litre engine which was followed by fifty other vehicles with their own prototype two litre chassis number sequence. Arthur recalls that the military were pushing for these kinds of improvements. Rover was responding as fast as it could, with orders flooding in from overseas and at home. A long wheelbase vehicle development vehicle soon followed. It was a curiosity with its dual features of load carrying and comfort. The team was aware of the lack of space in the 80" and that a proper load carrying vehicle was needed, hence, the long wheelbase development. They went down the path of making the vehicle more user friendly with this development. They used the front cab section of the recently introduced 'Tickford' bodied Land Rover Station Wagon and a large rear body, about twice the size of the standard Land Rover and with much deeper sides. The front springs of this vehicle were shackled the other way to the standard Land Rover. This inadvertently cured an intermittent minor wheel wobble problem that they had been trying to fix on the standard Land Rover for a while.

The engineers also built a test vehicle fitted with a 2.8 litre Rolls Royce B40 engine. Since the war, the British military wanted to develop their own more sophisticated version of the Jeep but development was very slow. Testing of the Rolls Royce engine was done initially in the Land Rover. This gave Arthur and his team an understanding of the engine and what engineering challenges they would have to address in using it with the Land Rover. They were confident about the Land Rover developments for the British Military. This was despite the facts that the Rolls engine alone cost as much as a single Land Rover and development of what was to become the Austin Champ was painfully slow.

Rover's own two litre engine testing was successful and led to the engine going into production in 1951. The torque of the two litre engine coming in at 1500 rpm was near perfect for an off road vehicle, and this led to the military's next request. They too felt the 80" Land Rover was too small, and they would like more space to try and accommodate six soldiers in the rear body rather than four. The next step was to start developing the 86" for the extra space required. Johnny Cullen once again led a lot of the development work for Arthur. This included an aluminium hardtop for the standard vehicle, as an option to replace the canvas top. Johnny felt that the rear body sides were too shallow for transporting people in the 80". The first 86" is similar to the long wheelbase with respect to both the body sides' depth and height. At first, the high sides did not quite work out on the 86" Land Rover, and production continued with the normal sides. Despite this, Arthur believes that the 86" was a truly great vehicle. With an extra nine inches of metal, the team had managed to increase the load carrying capacity of the vehicle by 25% and with this design created the opportunity for a number of future developments. They continued to use the 86" design as the basis for developing the long wheelbase vehicle. Rover introduced both for the 1954 season.

In early 1950s, Arthur was involved in a number of other Land Rover projects, including the Minerva. Arthur took great pleasure in working on the military aspects of the vehicles. He enjoyed the challenges they presented, such as waterproofing the petrol engines so that they could operate underwater. The Belgian military were looking for a fleet of vehicles, and Arthur became closely involved with the Minerva project. Minerva was a Belgian car manufacturer. Minerva was owned by Van Roggen and was tendering for a contract to assemble light 4x4 vehicles for the Belgian Ministry of National Defence. Rover won the contract, and Arthur was appointed the senior engineer from Rover in charge of Land Rover production. Van Roggen was a friendly chap and invited Arthur to visit his country house near Spa. Van Roggen's relationship with Rover turned sour over the terms of the contract and did not last long.

Arthur's involvement was usually one day per week at Minerva's factory in Morstel, approving all the changes that Minerva wanted to make to the Land Rover. These changes arose due to the tooling that the Morstel factory used. Gustaff Schmitt, an engineer, worked for Minerva. Schmitt's ability as an engineer and a multi-linguist inspired Arthur to appoint him as Chief Engineer for Rover's European activities. Arthur had so much work in England he could not keep a close eye on Belgian operations. Arthur especially liked the simple folded design for the Minerva's front mud guards. So Gustaff was obviously the right man at that time for the job.

Immediate post war Belgium and Europe were in the throes of reconstruction. Arthur remembers that steel was plentiful and that tax concessions varied across countries and markets. For example, depending on the country and the market, tax concessions could be awarded for supplying batteries and tyres and for the number of vehicles produced. Arthur recalls that in his first visit to the Minerva plant that it was so damaged from the war that he had thought to himself, 'They won't be making anything in this place. It's just a wreck." The factory was quickly rebuilt and producing. Minerva eventually manufactured more and more of the vehicles under licence from Rover and other CKD' plants began to appear in other European countries.

Military testing Spain in the early 1950's Arthur in the far right

Rover's ideas and Land Rover developments fell into place with the introduction of 86" and 107". Work on planning and design of the 86" started in late 1950 and the long wheelbase 107" in early 1949. These two models had long lead times and with the team's experience with the 80" they could anticipate the shortcomings of both vehicles. Unlike the 80" which had been literally thrown into production, the 86" would be a more disciplined affair. The less than ideal items in the 80" were ironed out and improved, including the 80" hood which flapped about and was very draughty, especially around the doors. The new models enabled the reintroduction of the Land Rover station wagon. Since 1948, Arthur had been very critical of the first Land Rover station wagon body from the traditional coach builders, Tickford of Newport Pagnell. The engineers knew the traditional timber coachwork would not be robust enough for the rough off road work. They had never pushed the vehicle terribly hard, even in testing.

Arthur acknowledges that the marketing people were right. The marketers had anticipated a market for a four wheel drive people carrying vehicle, and there most certainly was. The hardtop had been made for the 80" and was well into production by mid 1950, making a more viable people carrier for rough ground. The idea of a comfortable people carrier vehicle got a lot of thought. By the end of 1950, Land Rover discontinued production of the Tickford bodied station wagon. It sold well in certain export markets but the engineers believed it was a potential liability. The Tickford station wagon attracted sales tax in the UK market, and that made it incredibly expensive in the home market.

At this point, the Rover car side of the company started to consider an idea called the "Road Rover". The idea was essentially a more comfortable people carrying Land Rover station wagon. A mock up was made. Arthur's colleague Gordon Bashford did considerable work on the Road Rover that led to a number of two wheel drive prototypes being made. The Land Rover side was planning on reintroducing the Land Rover Station Wagon with the 86" and 107" based on the hardtop version of the standard Land Rover. After many years of production, the engineers were confident in the Land Rover's chassis strength, such that they could use if for almost any wheelbase. Arthur and his team assembled a number of chassis frames to enable coachwork companies to produce the right body for the people carrying Land Rover and the forward control chassis. Many ideas were tested on the Road Rover idea and the new Land Rover station wagon. At this point in the mid 1950s, the Rover engineers were operating at full Capacity and could not take on a development project of the size of the Road Rover. It required a suspension system suitable for carrying people in comfort. They knew that the old style off road vehicle leaf springs on the Land Rover chassis were not the ideal choice for transporting people. In the end the 86" and 107" station wagon were the best compromise at that time for this type of vehicle.

They Found Our Engineer

Prototype concept of the Land Rover 'Station Car' from 1954

In 1954, stylist David Bache joined the design team. Maurice Wilks believed that styling and finesse was of the utmost importance. Wilks dedicated many hours on getting the right colours, fabrics and finish. This was not an area that a hardened engineer like Arthur cared for or thought about much. Arthur loved working on Land Rovers. The Land Rover was an engineer's dream vehicle. You did not have to workout how to hide the crucial but ugly parts, like spot welds, seams, joints and rivets. For the Rover cars, engineers would often be at pains trying to resolve how to hide structural joints to make a seamless design work structurally and attractively. When called to see Maurice Wilks, Arthur was always a touch concerned that Wilks would present to Arthur a styling based engineering problem for his team to resolve. Arthur recalls that Wilks and Bache were in their element and both quickly set sight on "styling" the Land Rover.

Bache contributed a simple and effective styling idea for widening the high sided 86" prototype. The style idea was to extend the curve on the front outer wing panels for the full length of the vehicle below the top edge of the door and rear body lines. This had the effect of cleaning up to the lines of the Land Rover completely. They numerous ideas over the years for station wagons, high and low sided short wheelbase vehicles and for the high and low sides on the long wheelbase pickups had made some of the vehicles look a touch cobbled together for bits. This new styling idea would fix all these issues and with the Wilks brothers in charge, the idea was quickly approved. Arthur was concerned that widening the vehicle would cause problems for some of the Land Rover customers. Arthur had done extensive field testing in a number of countries with senior military officials and knew a wider vehicle, even just a couple of inches, might cause potential problems in tight off road and also vehicle storage situations

During this next phase of vehicle development initially called the Mark 2, Girling, a subsidiary of the Lucas electrical empire and the leading automative brake manufacturer of its' day, approached Arthur. Girling enticed Arthur with the post of technical director, a position on the Lucas Girling Board and higher pay. Tempted, Arthur left Rover in 1957. As Girling were based in Birmingham and a major supplier of Rover, Arthur initially stayed in close contact with developments at Rover. Arthur's assistant chief engineer job at Rover was split into two. Colonel Jack Pogmore became the engineer in charge of Land Rovers, and Chris Goode was in charge of Rover cars. Both still reported directly to the chief engineer Robert Boyle.

Since 1950, Land Rover had consistently outsold the Rover cars by a ratio of two to 1. It was now well established as Rover's core product line. Arthur became very familiar with his successor Jack Pogmore. Pogmore was a military man with a background in vehicle procurement, not an engineer. When Arthur left Rover, the design of the Land Rover was cast in stone for decades to come. Much of that original design is evident in the Defender today. At Pogmore's behest, he and Arthur often met. Pogmore used these meetings to ask questions on how and why the Land Rover had development the way it did.

By 1960 Arthur had settled in at Girling and never looked back. He worked with Rover on the brakes of the BRM Gas Turbine racing car. In the late 1960s, Rover made significant investments in developing the Range Rover, and Arthur met Spen King to discuss Girling brakes. In the 1970s, Arthur was offered a job in Sydney, Australia to manage the Girling/Lockheed joint venture that manufactured Girlock brakes for the Australian car industry. The joint venture was struggling. Arthur accepted the role and was able to turn the company around.

The engineering story behind the Land Rover now all started to make perfect sense. The questions remained. How did Arthur go missing? And given the huge interest in the Land Rover marque in the 1990s and 2000s, how did he remain missing? An answer to the questions lay with the fact that in the 1970s, Arthur was living twelve thousand miles and two decades away from the Land Rover's simple beginnings. By the 1970s, Rover was now part of British Leyland. The enthusiast scene for collecting and restoring the early Land Rovers grew significantly in Britain in the mid 1970s, with plenty of old farming and ex military vehicles and spares available. By the mid 1960s, the Wilks brothers had both died and Robert Boyle retired. A second answer is therefore that there were no remaining senior managers to tell the overall story. So the full story of the first Land Rovers could not be told and only parts of the story were known. It was a story awaiting to be told in full.

One of Arthurs test Land Rovers being loaded onto a freight airplane for testing in Europe with Arthur looking on

How do you find someone that you do not know is missing?

It is a strange question. The more one thinks about it, the more one goes around in a circle. Often the 'missing' person does not even realise that they are. Hard to believe, but that is what happened. Arthur did not know that he was missed and that a vital part of the Land Rover history was missing. To be truthful, Arthur was not actually found. It is more accurate to write that he was stumbled upon. Alex Massey and I did not realise this until we really started looking. For this story to miraculously unfold, it required people from across the world, previously unknown to each other, to cross paths. Unbelievable, but that is how it happened. Yet, in some ways, it did not "just happen" and, still, good fortune played its part in the crossings and connections.

'Let the vehicles tell you their secrets' has always been my motto. My collection of early Land Rovers and my articles in the Land Rover Register's (1948 to 1953) *'Full Grille'* attests to this. If you look closely enough, all the clues will be revealed. I had never contemplated meeting members of the original design team fifty to sixty years after the original events took place. *'Full Grille'* often led the way in early discoveries in the Land Rover world. It consists of a small and dedicated group of enthusiasts who not only have not only a deep knowledge on early Land Rover history, but also have many unanswered questions about Land Rovers early years.

Old Land Rovers are a fun bit of kit for the home motoring enthusiast. From the beginning, Land Rover was marketed as the 'versatile vehicle.' It allowed owners to adapt their Land Rover to meet their personal needs and interests. The perfectionist collectors can search for and find the perfect nut and bolt, complete an immaculate restoration, and polish the Land Rover every Sunday. Land Rovers are also perfect for those who just want a runabout to go to the shops on the weekend, do a bit of clearance or some minor farming. It also satisfies those who want to go off the beaten track, explore and travel in remote areas. And for those who want to do some farming, there is the power take off equipment to run farming equipment. The 'Meccano set' like simplicity lends itself to mechanics of all skills and interests.

The circumstances surrounding Arthur's reappearance start back in the mid 1970s with the Series 1 era Land Rovers. These are the Land Rovers with the flat sides on the main bodywork. By the mid 1970s, Series Ones represented a bygone time of the late 1940s and 1950s. People started looking and asking what had happened with the Land Rover. This interest spawned both the Land Rover Register 1948 to 1953 and the Land Rover Series One Club. Historical and technical information was very limited, with the "Register" leading the chase to uncover the history of the first 48 pre production models.

My own interest in the history developed as a teenager. From an early age, I was fascinated by anything that generated its own power. My grandfather and uncle farmed beef cattle in the hills east of Melbourne, Australia on the edge of Victorian high plains. A mid 1950s grey Ferguson tractor took us uphill and down dale on the farm. By the time I was 13, I felt the tractor was slow and was not as cool as having a four wheel drive. Unfortunately, the rest of my family were not interested in machinery and were not initially supportive of my idea to get a four wheel drive. Because of my young age, I was not allowed to drive, only to tinker with the farms modern vehicles. So I was on my own. Motivated to get my own runabout, I got a job delivering morning newspapers near home. At the newsagent, I read 4 x 4 magazines as well as the ads in the local "Melbourne Trading Post", looking for a cheap off road vehicle. This was the late 1980s. I was struck by what seemed a never ending stream of old Land Rovers in the paper. They were all early models too, from the late 40s and early 50s. Often, there were up to a dozen new ads each week, most of which were just affordable for a paper boy.

The "Melbourne Trading Post" came out on Thursday. It was delivered to the newsagent where I worked in the morning after I had left for school. To make sure that I did not miss an issue, I organised my Thursday tram ride home with precision. The school's finishing bell was at 3.30 pm. My bag was packed ready outside the door of the last class. I sat at the back of the room closest to the door and when that bell rang I was off like a rocket to catch the 3.36 pm No 64 tram, a twenty minute ride to the paper shop. If I ran, I made it. Sure, I may have missed some mischief hanging about with my mates, but I was not going to miss that opportunity of being able to buy the right Land Rover!! In contrast to my homework, I studied the Land Rover history with enthusiasm. I went to the local library and read up about them in the Graham Robson book, *'Land Rover, Workhorse of the World'* and knew I wanted an early 80" model. These small early vehicles were fascinating to me and much better than that slow old tractor on the farm. The basic Land Rover story that Maurice Wilks had 'found his Jeep so useful on the farm and hence came up with the Land Rover' was exactly what I wanted to hear.

My first 1950 80" Land Rover on a run in the Otway Ranges to the west of Melbourne in the mid 1990's

Persistence paid off and I eventually bought a Land Rover when I was 14 years old. Buying it took what seemed a frustrating amount of time. Once the tram arrived at the Paper shop, I would jump off, grab the paper, look quickly to see what vehicles were for sale and run home to call them up and find mostly that, "Sorry the Land Rover is sold". It seemed to happen every time until one day I got one. I dragged Mum and Dad up to Flowerdale just north of Melbourne. I had managed to get an early 1950 model. She looked very original but I did not know that fully then. It had been pulled apart by the owner to restore, but the owner had lost interest in the project and decided to sell it. So at the age of fourteen, I took on the task of putting this vehicle back on the road. I had always been quite good and interested in repairing things, but I was running quite blind on many things. Nonetheless, Mum and Dad were happy for me to do it.

Despite Dad's family having very little interest in machinery, my mechanical curiosity, unknown to me at the time, came from my mother's father who came from a small village outside Perth in Scotland. Mum had emigrated to Australia as a teenager with Gran, who was a true Londoner. My mother's parents had met when Gran worked in a Boots Pharmacy in London during the war. My grandfather came from Scotland to London to join the RAF and was a practical and talented home mechanic working on all sorts of machinery. However not everything works out sometimes and sadly my grandparents divorced. My grandfather returned to Scotland, and Gran and Mum emigrated to Australia. Both missed England terribly, so for them, the Land Rover was a piece of home.

The day arrived. We brought my first Land Rover home. I started getting into like a boy possessed. I joined the local Land Rover Owners Club of Victoria. They were fantastic in helping me out. The club librarian at the time, Anthony Maeder had a great 80" collection and had started his collection when he was young. He showed me what I needed to know about early Land Rovers and I managed to join one the Land Rover Register in England! I started writing letters and asking questions to the club's secretary. As I got to know the scene better, after school I rode my bike to the local Land Rover dealer, ULR, and looked at the exploded diagrams of the early Land Rover parts book in the spare parts department. I found my vehicle was extremely original. She had all matching numbers but still no one could answer my questions on the fine detail. As the parts book often showed something else I wondered, why was this part like this? And that part like that? I must have driven the staff there nuts.

Unknown to me at the time was that my early 1950 vehicle was a CKD, or Completely Knocked Down version. CKD's were sent out as a pack of six vehicles in major component sections. It was assembled by Regent Motors, at the bottom of Mt Alexander Road, along side Moonee Ponds Creek on the other side of town. In the early 1950s, Australia had large deliveries of Solihull built Land Rovers and CKD plants in a few Australian states. Many of the early features and odd items of these initial CKD vehicles were completely unknown amongst the local enthusiasts in Melbourne, as well as those back in England who had never seen the CKDs before. This all seemed part of a huge unknown mystery and was intriguing. So I kept writing and reading. I was sixteen and writing articles on the Land Rover Series 1 for the Victorian club As well as writing about Land Rovers and rebuilding Land Rovers, I looked out for and collected as many old factory service bulletins, owners manuals, photos and sales advertisements as I could.

I managed to get my Land Rover on the road when I was eighteen. This was thanks to plenty of help from the guys in the club, who would point me in the right direction. Overall the rebuild was not too difficult though I still had a lot to learn. I went onto to establish a collection of some very rare models. The height of the collection came early. I bought the 1950 model mobile welder when I was twenty. It was complete wreck. To this day, it one the earliest mobile welders in existence, despite the huge interest in the early vehicles now. Next was a 'holy grail'- a 1948 model. One from the very first year of production!

It is amazing how one thing can lead to another. Early vehicles, or at least rumours of them, came from all over the place. I was the registrar for the Australian Register List and maintained the official list of early Land Rovers known to still in be existence. It was certainly interesting and one got to know where and who had the interesting and rare items. For real research, however; I was frustrated. Australia is vast. To find rare vehicles, knowing what vehicles had been built and how many came here was vital.

The process of recording Land Rover data for the very early Pre Production vehicles was already in place in England and much data had been recorded. Tony Hutchings, the founder of the Land Rover Register, had written a Land Rover 'bible' in the 1980s 'Land Rover, The Early Years.' In this book, he described each of the 48 Pre Production vehicles and listed the known history about each vehicle, including what happened to each vehicle, by the time of book's publication. Hutchings accounted for some 20 of the 48 Pre Productions.

In the 1990s, two fellow members of the Victorian Club starting posting Land Rover information on the internet being almost the first to do so. They were Lloyd Allison and Anthony Maeder. At that time, both worked at Melbourne's Monash University in computer science. They encouraged me to publish online a paper that I had written on vehicle development changes on the 80" Land Rover. In 1996, I posted the paper on the internet on Lloyds 4wdonline.com web site documenting detailed vehicle changes for the first 80" model which became extremely popular.

Land Rover's 50th anniversary in 1998 inspired more enthusiasts to get connected. More and more early Land Rovers were accounted for and were

They Found Our Engineer

being restored. A number of new books were published on Land Rover's history and on restoring old Land Rovers. Glossy magazines were now available each month in store on Land Rovers in the UK and worldwide. Curious to know more, I delved into old workshop manuals and Hutchings' "Early Years." I was searching for clues to answer engineering mysteries about the earliest vehicles. I wanted to understand the complete history of the old Land Rovers, including who at Rover had used them and where the Land Rovers currently were. With respect to the finer details, The 48 Pre Production vehicles and the production models are quite different. These differences raised more questions about the development of the Land Rover that could not be answered by anything published so far. In its early years, the Land Rover continued to evolve at a rapid pace with an incredible number of improvements as it evolved.

I became completely absorbed in researching Land Rover's early history. The names of the people involved with the first 48 Pre Production vehicles gradually sank into my subconscious. I kept digging further and further into how the Land Rover was made and what vehicles were imported to Australia. I now was in my twenties, and travelling the world. I had the luxury of doing research at the British Motor Industry Heritage Trust Museum (BMIHT) at Gaydon in Warwickshire. A mere 30 minutes from Lode Lane, BMIHT holds factory dispatch information for the early Land Rovers. By this stage, I was obsessed. Obsessed with the early vehicles, and obsessed with restoring them. Knowing what exactly went to Australia was my main aim. By looking through the old records, I found out that various vehicles had been sent to the Rover development or engineering departments during Land Rover's early production years. These vehicles, no doubt, were to be tested or made into special prototypes. In these records, I saw a name that I had seen before in the "Early Years" book alongside Pre Production development vehicle number 36, but until now had not had any significance. The old records repeatedly showed that a certain individual received a number of very interesting development vehicles throughout Land Rover's early years. This person was Mr Arthur Goddard.

The Boy from the Outback

The Australian Outback is not just Alice Springs or Ayres Rock. Australia is vast. Outside its' main cities, populations are small, with the long distances between settled areas. These distances are unimaginable to people who live in more densely populated countries. In Australia, many places are way, way 'outback.' Young Alexander Massey comes from Clermont in North Central Queensland, some 600 miles from the Queensland capital Brisbane. By anyone's book, it is out there.

The area rises from Emerald (elevation 169 metres). It forms a tear drop shape to the north, encompassing Capella in the middle and Clermont (elevation 267 meters), some 60 miles to the northwest of Emerald. The fantastic rise in the landscape entices rain away from North western Australia to fall in this remote area of Queensland. Europeans, attracted by the agricultural potential, settled in the area from the 1860s. They first explored the Clermont Region in Queensland's Central Highlands in 1845. Ludwig Leichhardt explored the area as part of his expeditions into central and northern Australia. Clermont's main industries are coal mining and farming.

In post war British Commonwealth countries, like Australia, you can bet that where there is farm, there will also be Land Rovers. This area of Queensland, no doubt, imported the early Land Rovers, starting from their "birth" in 1948. In the early 1950s, with the aim of ending wartime food rations, the British government set up the Overseas Food Corporation (OFC) to increase food production in British Commonwealth countries. The idea was to have a variety of large broad acre farming projects to mass produce certain crops. A number of OFC activities were put in place, one of the best known was in Africa, the Tanganyika ground nut scheme. On a similar basis, the Queensland State Government created the Queensland British Food Corporation (QFBC) to produce sorghum.

Started in 1948, the QBFC initially had just over 92,500 acres in cultivation. By 1949, this increased to 492,171 acres (199,182ha) of land across the Central Highlands. The properties extended from west of Rolleston to Cullin-La-Ringo and Marmadilla, south of Emerald, to Peak Downs and Retro at Capella to Wolfgang, north of Clermont. To cover these vast areas, vehicles were brought in en mass. By 1950, the QBFC had huge fleets of hundreds of farming vehicles and machinery, including Land Rovers. Like the African schemes, the plans quickly ran into huge problems with pests and drought. By 1953 the scheme was being wound up, with plots of land sold to local farmers. Unlike the African schemes, farms that formed much of the original stations are still being farmed today, and the Land Rovers were there to stay.

Australian enthusiasm for motor vehicles runs thick in the heart of the country. This passion has resulted in a "war" between owners of locally made Ford and General Motors-Holden cars. From this one eyed love of a make, model and marque, a whole motorsport industry in Australia has boomed. A Ford or Holden man of the 70s and 80s in Queensland drove a vehicle for use on the land. You were either a Land Rover man or a Toyota Land Cruiser man. No ifs or buts. Back in 1950s; however, in Queensland and Melbourne alike, it was Land Rovers only. There was no other four wheel drive that compared.

As a child, Alex Massey was obsessed with diggers, tractors and farm machinery. His family had been in Clermont since the 1890s and knew everyone. Alex's father Russell was an apprentice at his father's garage in Clermont. The garage was established in the early 1950s and was first a Volkswagen dealer and later sold the Australian made Chrysler Valiant. In the 1960s, the American car manufactures had a strong presence in Australia. Yet, it was often said that "The Holden and Ford 6 cylinders and V8s were big, but Valiant's were Bigger." If you had the best Aussie car, you had a Valiant.

The isolation and rigour of the 'outback' demands that little is wasted. Clermont's centenary was in 1964 and celebrate early motoring in the Clermont Region, the Massey garage brought a few old cars from the outback stations to show at the Clermont's centenary parade. Alex's Gran knew of some early Vauxhalls down the road in Paddy Houston's Yard. She managed to convince old Paddy into letting her have a vehicle for her husband to restore. Paddy insisted that the vehicle remained original. It was a very old, pre 1920s vehicle which they were able to get the back to Clermont. It had been sold new to a Mr James Tolson of the Glenmore Downs station some 45 miles outside of town. The Vauxhall had not moved much since the great 1916 Queensland Flood, when it was brought to Clermont to be serviced. It was completely submerged in the flood. The car was nearly 100% complete except for the radiator motif which was quite a unique piece. Whilst the Rolls Royce 'Spirit of Ectasy' mascot on the huge Edwardian radiators was relatively commonplace, the Vauxhall's hissing cat, known as the 'swearing cat,' was not. Local legend was that a local quiet 'tinker' type person in the town had taken the swearing cat years ago. Keen on local history and with the local myths and rumours in mind, Alex's Gran was determined to get the cat back. She purchased a bottle of rum and swapped the rum for the swearing cat. Almost complete, the Vauxhall needed a few parts. Correspondence was entered into with the Vauxhall Motor company in England, who were pleased to hear of such an early model. Vauxhall confirmed that it was a 1913 16/20 model and supplied a new water pump, which was essential in getting the vehicle going again.

The second old vehicle for the Clermont centenary parade was a local Ford Model T which was a mere 120 miles ways from Clermont. On inspection, the timberwork and the whole Model T was completely rotten and the Masseys were dismayed to discover that it needed so much work. Their disappointment quickly disappeared, as they were soon offered another local car - a 1930 Ford Model A in running condition. The Model A was used to cart feed and had a fascinating history. It was known as the 'Green Goblin.' Shirley Lay, a Brisbane traveller, had driven the "Green Goblin" around the whole of Australia. She wrote a book about her travels, in which the Green Goblin played a major part.

Motoring history was now in the Massey families' veins. Their Clermont garage had sold cars that were just the usual run of the mill main steam VW's and Chrysler's, but the old the Vauxhall and the Green Goblin's were now firmly part of the fabric that made up the Massey Garage. These two cars history became part of their family history. Born in 1988, Alex from an early age had a strong appreciation of local and vehicle history. In time, Alex's father moved on from N.W Massey and Co. For a brief period, Russell worked at New Track which sold Versatile tractors. He then moved to an automotive spare parts business and eventually moved to Brisbane.

As a child, Alex tinkered with the toy cars, trucks and tractors. The father of his friend Andrew Cruickshank had a roadworks and grader business and a share in a farm in the 7000 plus acre Aroa Downs station. The farm was relatively small for the area as it was an arable farm, it did not need the acreage required for cattle. The vast machinery sheds at Aroa housed almost everything for crop work. As the boys reached 7 years old, 'The Shed' at the station became their toy box with huge life sized toys. Being outback lads with a spirit of adventure and almost limitless private space, looking at the machines was not as much fun as starting and driving the various tractors, harvesters and trucks at the station. These huge vehicles are cumbersome for anyone to drive, let alone lads of around seven. The boys quickly realised the fun in the fields was to be had in the cars or even better, in the four wheel drives.

Andrew took a shine to the Toyota Land Cruisers. Alex was hooked on the quirky old Land Rovers that had been there forever and a day. One day, the local gentlemen's clothing store manager, who knew the family well, gave Alex a copy of the 'Brookland's 1948 to 1973 Land Rover Road Tests' booklet to read and enjoy. Alex was glued to the pages and became truly as obsessed as only a boy could be. He had never seen any of the very early late 1940 Land Rovers, and the fascination and obsession grew. For Land Rover's 50th anniversary in 1998, 10 year old Alex even had his mum bake a Land Rover shaped cake for the celebrations.

By the early 1990s, though numerous, many of the old 1950s Land Rovers were tired and run down. They were much loved despite later divisions in modern 4x4 make allegiances. Alex was besotted with the old Land Rovers and looked out everywhere for them. With the arrival of his brother and sister, the growing family moved to Brisbane. City life offered new opportunities, yet the Massey family maintained strong connections with friends and family in Clermont. Missing the station and the luxury of space to play with vehicles, computers became Alex's great interest. Nonetheless, once Alex was within a whisker of being driving age, the interest in the old Land Rovers re-ignited. He had to have one.

The car collection also made the move to Brisbane from Clermont. The jewel of the collection, the 1913 Vauxhall was first. Nearly 100 years old, she is a very collectable Edwardian age car that Russell would restore for its' second time. Alex got a 1953 80" Land Rover on ebay from near Toowoomba to restore and get going. As we all know, often one Land Rover is not enough for a car mad family. Back at Clermont, Alex and Russell rescued the next project. It was a 1951 model 80" that had been on the Paradise Downs Station and was one of the earliest found in that area so far. This particular Land Rover had a touch of character about her. For years, she been used for wild pig hunting and was lovingly named 'Leaping Lil' by all that knew her.

'Leaping Lil', Alex's 1951 80" Land Rover being made ready for the move to Brisbane and the first early Land Rover Arthur had seen in decades

Leaping Lil made the move down to Brisbane too. Due to lack of space at home, Russell decided to store Lil at his workshop with the antique Vauxhaul. Russell's workshop is on a business estate with dozens of other businesses and warehouses. Towards the end of 2006, a trailer firm, Vehicle Components, which specialises in off road trailer components, moved to the business estate just over the road from Russell's business. The owner of the company was unknown to Russell or Alex. He was one Arthur Goddard, the former Assistant Chief Engineer of Rover in Solihull.

Mountains of Information

This research has taken many years, and it was not the work of one person alone. Over the years, many Series One enthusiasts have discovered bits and pieces of information that have added to the fascinating store about what had really happened at Rover. My friends in the Register all knew that something was missing in the story. Every now and then someone else would report in *'Full Grille'* or the Series 1 clubs *'Legend'* that this or that piece of information had been found. These discoveries always added to the core knowledge with the now clubs. Sharing what we uncovered, we knew that the early Land Rover did not 'just happen' and that there was more to the Land Rover than its' appearance on 30 April 1948 at Amsterdam.

From 'The Times' Feb 28 1948,
CAR MANUFACTURERS SIDELINES. KEEPING WORKS OPEN
From our Motoring Correspondent. Coventry, Feb 27

Motor firms in the Midlands are divided in their reactions to the Government's method of allocating steel supplies in accordance with export performance.

Some makers of high-grade cars are confident that they can reach an export trade that will satisfy the Government on monetary grounds, although it may not be the proportion of output (three-quarters) mentioned as a general quota, and that they can safely continue to concentrate on making cars. Others have decided that, even with a reasonable export trade, it may be necessary to manufacture additional products in order to keep their factories working at an economical rate.

One of the most interesting sidelines being developed is a new vehicle for farmers, who have shown, by their wide spread use of American jeeps acquired from Government depots, the need for a vehicle of this type that can be taken across country with out being damaged or becoming bogged.

Snippets of information such as this were always appearing in The Register's magazine. These snippets generated more curiosity about the Land Rover story, inspired further articles, and encouraged further research to build a greater level of understanding for those who were just hooked on trying to discover what the truth was about the Land Rover.

For me, a young person and with UK heritage, going back and forth from there to Australia did not present any problems. The main challenges were the time and required focus it took to comprehend all these pieces of disparate information. The early vehicle development did not stop when Land Rover went into production. All sorts of interesting sidelines could be researched, which is all very addictive for an obsessed enthusiast. The great part about researching a car company is that vehicles and racing go hand in hand. This hunt for information is in many ways like a car race. It is a race for the next find, clue or discovery of a missing, photo, part, manual or vehicle or some crazy piece of information in the long lost rare Early Owners Manual. Like any race, especially involving cars or vehicles, it can get insanely competitive amongst the other enthusiasts and mates you are racing against.

Since the initial development of the vehicles over sixty years ago, the Rover Company had changed hands and departments had moved. Often machinery and documentation was misplaced, lost or just thought not important anymore and disposed of. The more that we enthusiasts looked at the available information about the romantic story of Land Rovers and the Centre Steer, the less sense it made. For example, it was always said the Land Rover was just supposed to be the stop gap until Rover cars got back to the level of sales they had before the Second World War. The closer; however, one looks at the very early Land Rovers in production order, it becomes obvious that early on more and more pressed mass production parts were added to the vehicles. This all takes huge amounts of tooling to be made and requires significant investment. By the end of 1948, the British military had tested two Pre Productions and took receipt of a small batch of production vehicles. This was followed by a huge batch of vehicles to the military in 1949. In addition, the Indian Army took receipt of two very early production models for evaluation. Something in the uncovered history still was not quite right. Further information was needed to explain the full story.

They Found Our Engineer

Goddard and Cullen putting *Huey* through its paces in 1948

Tom and his father Guy are two of my great specialist mates. They are just as crazy as myself about the factory owned Land Rovers and are very fascinated with early development vehicles. In the 1960s, Guy did his motor apprenticeship at Coxeter's, the Rover dealership in Oxford. At that time, Series One Land Rovers of 40s and 50s were still relatively new. Guy has a great deal of factory service knowledge that is invaluable in the garage as well as researching. In 2006, Tom came across another former factory vehicle still in existence- a left hand drive 1951 model. We suspected that this was a test vehicle for a huge batch of Belgian military based CKD vehicles assembled by Minerva in Antwerp. Once again a great 'excuse' to visit the British Motor Heritage Trust Museum at Gaydon, and trawl through the old Rover Company dispatch books. Like many others, the vehicle had been dispatched to Arthur Goddard. We were on a bit of a roll with this vehicle, as the photo of another factory vehicle of around the same age as the Minerva trials in the early 50s had also very recently reappeared. We looked that one up and once again it was also sent to Goddard. That piece of information combined with the knowledge that we had about the large list of development vehicles he received from 1948 to 1951, firmly placed his name in my mind as someone who was important at Rover. Still, no one knew anything about him. Somehow he had been missed from the history so far. Curiosity about what he had done – yes, but where he fits in the story so far? We had not much to go on. It was information to store away for later use. It was clear that a few pieces of this puzzle were still missing.

The Final Pieces of the Jigsaw.

Life moves on. I did have a bit of a life besides old Land Rovers. Now married and running my own business, my wife and I had the chance to move to the UK. I had a unique opportunity to introduce an Australian company to the UK, and my wife Michelle has a career in genetics education that keeps her more than busy.

At the time of our move to the UK, Julian, another great mate, and I purchased a 1948 Pre Production vehicle, number 16. It was one of the 48 initial trial 'pre production' vehicles Rover made. I had looked at it with fascination for so many years. I had a hunch that 16's history would be exceptionally good. Number 16 had stayed at the Solihull factory's service department as a works hack for all its' working life. She was in extremely good condition and very nice too on the originality stakes. I had helped the previous owner put her back on the road in a rush before the Land Rover 50th Birthday in 1998, so knew the car inside out. We bought her just in time for Julian and I to take her to the 60th Birthday celebrations in 2008.

Now living England, I started to trace 16's life back in the factory. As luck would have it, a time came when I was again at the Heritage archives, which by now I was very familiar. My plan was to first to look for old photos of the Rover works, with the hope that 16 would be in some of them. The archivists are a great help at Gaydon and really appreciate enthusiasts' knowledge too. For this research they suggested that I contact Roger Crathorne. He had worked at Rover and Land Rover for years. He was the Heritage museum that day. The archivists called him there and then, assured that he would know the vehicle.

Roger's career started as an apprentice at Land Rover in the early

Michael Bishop

1960s. He came a development engineer on the original Range Rover project and a world renowned specialist in off road driving. Known as the current 'Mr Land Rover,' I knew of Roger but didn't want to waste his time with a 'mad enthusiast's wild goose chase'. In light of my reluctance, the friendly archivists insisted that this kind of information was one of Roger's specialties, and they called him to the Archive Reading Room. Roger duly appeared and introduced himself. I mentioned the vehicle and the trade plate number that 16 had used at Rover - 260AC. He immediately understood what I was saying and knew the vehicle well. It transpired that 16 was the first vehicle he had driven back in his early days at the factory and off road too. Many of the apprentices back then had learnt to drive a Land Rover in the old service department hack. He was delighted to know that she had survived. This was unbelievable! My hunch on 16's Rover history, or '260' as I found she was called at Rover, proved right and much better than I had expected. After sharing a few more tales of '260' towing trailers, collecting workshop manuals from the printers, and also enjoying fish and chips for Friday lunch with the boys in the service department, Roger handed me his card and said to keep in touch. So I did.

I called Julian at work and shared what had just transpired with Roger. He was stunned. As 16's part owner, he was half cursing that he wasn't there for the excitement of a great historic find, but also pushing me to find more. I emailed Roger some pictures I had of '260' unrestored and thanked him for his time. I was always up for new discoveries and was accustomed to how they could just happen out of the blue. In no way, however, could I have anticipated who would appear next and where he would be found.

The Patience of Youth

Age and memories play tricks on you. Watching as the next generation goes through the same experiences as you can be very enlightening. I first came across Alex from an Australian Early Land Rover email distribution list. This was in mid 2000 while I was still living in Australia. He was looking for a bulkhead for his 1953 80" Land Rover. This is the main body frame. Made from mild steel, the bulkhead is attached to the doors, bonnet, mudguards, dashboard, and steering and houses the main wiring for the electrical system. It is an essential part of the vehicle. In Australia, they are called "firewalls" due to the heat of the engine from the other side to the cab.

Alex was young and keen, trying to learn as much as he could. I was collecting this part to send back to England where they rust away badly due to the constant damp and harsh winter environment. They had become almost impossible to find in England. Given that 27,000 Series 1 Land Rovers had been exported to Australia, a good one can be found in the drier parts of the county without too much trouble. Seeing similarities in how our interest in Land Rovers started in our youth and wanting to encourage Alex in his interest, I sold him a particularly good "firewall". Land Rover's 60th anniversary was in 18 months' time, and Alex was so young, keen and excited to have his Land Rover on the road for this great event. I had been much the same at his age and had benefited from help that I had received from friends and fellow enthusiasts. Helping Alex was just something I wanted to do.

Brisbane is a thousand miles from Melbourne. Anthony Maeder one of the Land Rover enthusiasts who had helped me heaps as a teenager, also lived in Brisbane. As both were living in Brisbane, Anthony and Alex

Michael Bishop

would get together to discuss and look around Anthony's Land Rovers. Given their relationship, I was very confident that the part would be put to good use.

The Australian 60th Land Rover anniversary event was held in Cooma, in the heart of the Snowy Mountains. The 1950s Snowy Mountains Hydro Electric Scheme had been built with a huge fleet of Land Rovers. Land Rovers are still synonymous with the Snowy Scheme's history and the area of the greater Monaro Region of New South Wales. I had my two early 80" vehicles ready for the drive to Cooma and was very busy with the impending move to the UK. In Cooma I met Alex and his dad Russell for the first time. Tom Pickford had travelled from England to attend the celebrations, as had many other mates from all over Australia and New Zealand.

Young Alex was doing well. His vehicle had made it there. He was keen to learn and had an enthusiast's desire to learn more. At the gala dinner evening, he was on our table. Over a few glasses of red wine, I had a great chat with Russell about restoring vehicles, youth, car clubs and so on. They were good company. I was quietly pleased that I had done the right thing in helping a young enthusiast.

Being busy and focussing on my new life in England, I didn't have time to think about the significance of meeting Alex and Russell in Cooma. Michelle and I arrived in England. She settled in well at her job with the National Health Service (NHS). I was determined for once to not let my hobby dominate our lives and got down to the work of establishing UK operations for the Australian company. Still, I continued with my hobby and kept in touch with Land Rover friends. Eventually, at the request of the Series 1 club, I used the research that I had done in the mid 1990s for 4wdonline to update their web page. The Land Rover Register's *'Full Grille'* magazine needed a few articles too. The Register only prints five or six editions of *'Full Grille'* each year and is put together by Dave Hanson, a keen Land Rover enthusiast. Dave had discovered some fascinating information about the first Land Rover Road test that was done by journalists in the late 1940s, and was keen to share the story with the *'Full Grille'* readers.

One morning at my computer started to buzz with a Skype call from young Alex in Brisbane. It had been nearly a year since Cooma and was great to hear from him. Keen and full of excitement, he was running about doing this and that with the 53 model 80." Alex is a good talker at the best of times. It was morning in England and I was working, so I tried to keep the vehicle discussion as brief as I politely could. Another morning not long after, Alex called again, bursting with enthusiasm. A previously 'lost' 1948 model Land Rover was for sale in Australia. The holy grail of all Land Rovers for enthusiasts and number 855 off the line and should he buy it?

He was seeking my advice because I have owned many early Land Rovers over the years. But, in many ways this was a silly question to ask me. 'Of course you should buy it', was my answer. You don't get many opportunities to own these very collectable models. Alex rung off and and called back a half hour later. The deal was done; he had bought 855. The only thing was that 855 was in Sydney, 600 miles away from Brisbane - a 1200 mile round trip to collect and transport home.

Chassis R860855 was one of the first batch of ten vehicles despatched to the first New South Wales dealer, Grenville Motor's of Sydney. The sales books of Grenville Motor's are still in existence, and showed that R860855 was sold to A.A. Daglish in February 1949. It is still relatively easy to read the Daglish name and the farm station's area on the front driver outer mudguard of 855. Alex, much in the family tradition with the Vauxhall and Green Goblin, used the phone book and found the station. The Daglish family were still living on the station. John Daglish was 16 in 1949 and remembers the vehicle as a great one that served him well. Excitedly, Alex emails all this new information to me. It was great material, perfect for an article in *Full Grille*. I was impressed that the boy was learning and getting on so well.

The Masseys made the journey down from Brisbane to collect 855 over the weekend of 28/29 March 2009. Very soon after the trip, I had another internet call from Alex asking all sorts of questions. At this stage of the 80" Land Rover story, many of the features and details of an early 1948 vehicle like 855 were undocumented. During the early years of production and whilst moving to mass production, there were still a lot of handmade parts. Alex was keen to learn more, particularly unusual pieces of information. Once again, Alex called mid morning English time, while I was busy working. When I had some time, I called him back and answered his questions. He was so excited and was talking almost '14 to the dozen.' Completely out of the blue, Alex mentioned that his father's business is in Brisbane, that an engineer works just opposite and the engineer's name is Arthur Goddard who used to work at Rover in the 1940s and 50s.

Are you sure?

Upon hearing that name and knowing its context, I suddenly felt very curious and somewhat puzzled. I told Alex to hold on a second, so I could grab the definitive 'Early Years' book on the Pre Production vehicles and found "A.Goddard" once again as Pre Production 36's first custodian. Back to the computer, I asked Alex to grab his copy of the book, which he had just received from 'The Register' and to look at 36's dispatch details and A. Goddard.

"Is this person, the man you are talking about'" I asked.

"Yes I think so," answers Alex, having no idea of the implications of what he had just said. He then forwards me an internet link to a newsletter about Vehicle Components, which is a family run business that makes trailer axles. At 88 years old, Arthur is the head engineer of that company, having worked at Rover on cars and Land Rovers!

Everything started to happen quickly, so we put a quick plan together. Russell had already spoken to Arthur about Rover. As Brisbane is 10 hours ahead of England, Alex arranged to see Arthur Goddard the next day to try and find out a bit of what he knew. We had no idea how Arthur would respond or what he had done. We only knew that sixty years ago that he had been the recipient of a vast number of Land Rovers. Full of anticipation, young Alex was eager to learn as much as he could. I provided Alex with photographs and a brief list of questions. I suggested to Alex that he should take along a copy of the 'Early Years' to show pictures of early Land Rovers from the book. As a young enthusiast, he was as well equipped as he could be to speak with a person whom we would eventually discover was one of Land Rover's royalty.

They Found Our Engineer

Arthur and Alex in Alex's 1953 Land Rover,
outside the two Brisbane factories

Sixteen hours later, late in the evening UK time, Alex sent me a 45 minute video recorded interview with Arthur Goddard, the Rover Company Limited's assistant chief engineer from 1949 to 1957. We knew nothing about him. Arthur had started at Rover in 1944. What he said and recalled was pure Land Rover gold. Arthur spoke as though the job was done five years ago. He had amazing recall of fine detail from sixty plus years ago as well as a fantastic sense of humour.

Arthur shared his story with Alex. After Rover, he had moved to Lucas Girling for the majority of his career. He was initially technical director for Girling Brakes, then became the managing director of Automotive and Girling, a Girling and Lockheed subsidiary Australian brake manufacturer. In the 1980s, Arthur moved to Quinton Hazell Automotive in Australia. After that, he moved to his own engineering business in Australia specialising in caravan and off road trailer axles where he is still working as head engineer. Amazing.

I had this very strange feeling of disbelief. A huge dose of how did that happen? What had just happened? In Australia of all places too? Events like this don't just happen. It transpired that Alex had known of Arthur for a while, a couple of years in fact. His father's timber products business is just across the road from Goddard's trailer axle business. It was Russell restoring his 1913 Vauxhall at the factory that had caught Arthur's eye. For a short while, Alex had also kept the early Land Rover 'Leaping Lil' that he had rescued there. After seeing his first early Land Rover in decades, Arthur started to talk with Russell about cars and his days at Rover. Putting two and two together and realising Arthur's former position at Rover, Russell suggested to Alex that he had a chat with Arthur. When I was sixteen, I didn't listen to my parents and neither did Alex. Despite what his father said, Alex could not contemplate that the senior engineer team of the first Land Rover in 1948 was literally over the road, in Brisbane, Australia. As consequence not much happened until that Skype call took place on that fortuitous day a few years later.

I was close to speechless but had the sense to call two friends to share what had just happened. I called Tom first and then Dave Hanson who was always scratching around for more articles for the club magazine. Both were very surprised. I then contacted three people who are extremely well informed about Land Rover's history. The first person I contacted was John Smith who was in the last throws of finishing his book of 25 years, *Land Rover: The Formative Years*. I emailed him and received a message back to say 'unbelievable,' but unfortunately his book had just finally gone to press a few weeks ago. I then contacted my good friend Peter Galilee who writes detailed history articles for Land Rover Owner Magazine. He had helped me out a lot when he was the Register secretary and I was still a lad. He was in a hurry and much to my surprise just said "No." Undeterred, I got out my list of business cards and called Roger Crathorne at Land Rover.

Roger knew Arthur's name. He had seen Arthur's name on documentation, signing off various parts from the 1950s, but couldn't place him. I explained that Arthur had left Rover in around 1957, a number of years before Roger's time. I shared with Roger that Arthur had said that he had worked with all the big names at Rover. Surely Spen King would know Arthur. I asked Roger if I could please have Spen King's phone number. Helpful as ever, Roger obliged.

I pinched myself to make sure that this wasn't just a dream. Charles Spencer 'Spen' King is a huge name in British automotive engineering. He was the head of the original Range Rover project and has many other cars to his credit. As it happens, by chance a few years before, I came across and became very familiar with the first Australian Range Rover (which is another story). As a result, I knew a lot about Spen's career and despite he too being one of Rover's royalty, I felt that I would not embarrass myself if

I were to call him. Spen was great. He was now retired and he had known Arthur well. Spen said that he would be very happy to see me to chat about those days at Rover in the 1940s and 1950s.

It was very good of Spen to meet with me. He started with "You can ask me what you like but spare the Range Rovers. I've been asked all that before." Fair enough. When Arthur was working at Rover, Spen was working in the gas turbine department on jet cars. Spen had occasionally worked with Arthur, testing JET 1, Rover's first gas turbine powered car. Not surprising, he instantly knew Arthur had been in charge of the research laboratory. He knew that Arthur had been fortunate as a young engineer to become assistant chief engineer, which covered a vast engineering scope at Rover. He also knew that Arthur had moved to Girling as technical head. He believed that Arthur was now in Australia. The fact that Spen thought Arthur was in Australia really surprised me. From Spen's point of view, Arthur wasn't missing, but then again, no one had ever asked Spen about Arthur before. Spen went onto explain that he was always asked about his vehicles and not about his colleagues.

We had a fascinating chat about Rover. We talked about Spen's two uncles Spencer and Maurice Wilks and what it was like working in the family company. We chatted about gas turbines, jet engines and the Frank Whittle aero jet engine era during the Second World War. Our conversation covered various projects that didn't quite make it to production, such as the small post war M type car and early 50s Road Rover. Spen believed that the 1950s were Rover's 'Golden Days.' It was a fantastic place to work, and they all had a lot of fun. Often after the day's work was done, engineers would look to see what was being done in other departments. Spen remembered the famous first 'Centre Steer' Land Rover. In 1947, many Jeep parts were used to build the Centre Steer to evaluate the viability of the Land Rover idea. Spen recalls that it wasn't a great vehicle to drive. All the engineers took the opportunity to play about in it. Like any other engineering prototype, it was just a means to an end. It was great to confirm what many had suspected about the 'Centre Steer' from their piecing of the story together over the years.

It so happened that Spen's father also came from Melbourne. He lived not far from where I used to catch the 64 tram home from school, often dreaming of Land Rover and Range Rovers too!! Despite the number of books on the history of various areas of Rover, Spen felt that none of the books told the full story. Rover was a large and innovative company, working on numerous developments across different departments in which

Michael Bishop

many ideas and events overlapped. The history books to date 'never touched the sides' about what everyday working life was like at Rover during those heady times. History books focussed on a specific vehicle say the Series 1 Land Rover or P4 Rover Car. None of the books described the dynamics of Rover at the time in which these two vehicles were not only assembled side by side on the factory floor but mutually influenced the other's design.

Based on the information we had uncovered so far, I wrote an article for *'Full Grille'* that editor Dave Hanson thought was fantastic. The story focussed on finding Arthur and Arthur's recollections. I was really grateful and thanked Spen for his input. It was a real buzz to have been personally involved in discovering a totally new aspect of the Land Rover story. The story "connected the dots" by sharing Arthur's perspective on what happened and how it all fit together. We were in a full state of historic euphoria in putting the magazine together. We revelled in digging deeper and deeper into the complex chain of events from the 1940s. We were exhilarated in knowing that we were telling the full story for the first time.

I asked Alex to continue interviewing Arthur whenever he could, and set areas of interest that the interview should cover. Arthur was more than happy to keep talking, and on it went. Hour after hour of information came from Arthur. After reading the second club magazine article that we wrote about Arthur, Roger called me to say how much he was enjoying the articles. The articles had prompted Roger to ask Arthur about his recollections on some finer details.

Arthur had recently been talking to Alex about a test area that Rover had developed called the Belgian Pavé at the Motor Industry Research Association (MIRA) facilities. The rough test section of road replicated a rear section in Belgium. The road is made from cobblestones and over time becomes very uneven and with undue haste completely shook vehicles to bits. The replica road section was located at the MIRA facilities at Nuneaton, not far from Rover at Solihull. It was used to test suspension and body shell strength to the limit. Arthur had shared that he and Bro Ward had made the Pavé for Rover with export vehicle testing in mind. It proved to be perfect for testing the Land Rover. Arthur's recollections matched perfectly what had been previously cobbled together about the previously unheard Pave test track. Arthur's memories were like clockwork, in fact just like a perfectly tuned engine firing up and idling smoothly. When Roger tested the first Range Rover prototypes in the mid to late 1960s at MIRA, he had heard that a Land Rover engineer had helped make the Pavé, but no one could exactly recall who. We had the answer now. It was Arthur Goddard.

A few weeks later I heard from my local Worcester collector mate, Bob Jones. Bob had taken his 1948 model Land Rover to the Birmingham Classis Car show at the NEC Exhibition centre to display on the Land Rover Series One Club stand. He saw Roger at the show. Roger was looking at the historic vehicles on the club stands. Bob let me know that in thick of conversation, Roger had happily commented about the interesting pieces of Land Rover history that had recently reappeared and that "They had found our Engineer." It was no doubt now that Arthur really had been, so to speak, missing.

What we did find!!!

As far as Land Rover history was concerned, Arthur was not on the radar screen. The research team (Alex, Dave Hanson and I) carefully edited and cross checked the information that we collected from Alex's interviews with Arthur. Dave and I reread all that we could from the late 1970s and the 1980s when Land Rover's history was first being written in a comprehensive way. In rereading the material from various authors and experts from here and there, we found that people had not said anything that was inaccurate, nor did the other historians misrepresent what happened. It became evident that people were not clear about what had really happened. Certainly the 'stop gap' has its part in the Land Rover story, but previous stories were not clear about how long it was planned to remain just a stopgap. In addition, there was a void of information between the Centre Steer stage period and when the early pictures of number 01 (know as HUE or *Huey* from its registration) appeared in the newspapers in late April 1948.

Tony Hutchings started The Land Rover Register 1948 to 1953, and in the 1980s coined the term 'the missing link.' This term referred to the airbrushed photos of the centre steer vehicle that were carefully airbrushed to look like the real Land Rover for use in the first sales' brochures. It left us guessing at how had the Series One design evolved from what had been the Centre Steer vehicle? How were the developments of the two vehicles linked? Over the years, enthusiasts and historians had written many articles and letters on what they suspected may have happened at this 'missing link' stage. Given the void, it was a matter of using the information known so far. As small clues appeared, they were used to fill in some of the gaps and speculation was used to try to fill in the other gaps to determine what happened. Similar to the experience with the evolution from the Centre

Steer to the first Land Rover, information was equally as vague when the models changed from the 80" to the 86" and 107" and for the Series 2.

The unplanned crossing of paths across the world resulted in a new discovery about Land Rover's very early history. It was uncharted territory and Alex and Russell thought this was incredible. Suddenly, a new window was opened into the early history of the Land Rover. A window that went right back to the Second World War. It brought to light a previously hidden view into the world of Rover senior management during the Wilks' era of managing one of the British midlands' greatest car companies. In the days after Arthur appeared, I was in a trance-like state. It was as though all this information that I had spent so many years studying, much of which I could recall or find quite quickly, was suddenly all being rebooted, reprocessed and reorganised in my head. It was beyond comprehension that the senior engineer of the original 1948 team of a worldwide iconic vehicle and brand could be delivered to your front door ready to answer questions sixty odd years after the original work was done.

The recollections of other members of the old team were important too. I read again the interviews with various other members of Rover's senior engineers including Gordon Bashford and engine man Jack Swaine but couldn't find a solid link between them, the Land Rover project evolution and Maurice Wilks. It was Arthur and chief engineer, Robert Boyle, who reported to Maurice Wilks, who were missing. Tom Barton's recollections didn't include very much information about his former colleagues. As Spen King noted, people asked about the vehicles you worked on, not about your colleagues.

It now all seemed odd to me and raised further questions in my mind. Boyle had been at Rover a long time, despite a brief stint at Morris in Cowley before the war. Unfortunately for Rover historians, Robert Boyle shares his names with a 17th century philosopher and most internet researches on Robert Boyle yield information on Robert Boyle the philosopher, not Robert Boyle the chief engineer. Still lacking information on the apparent disappearance of these two senior men, Boyle and Goddard, it was left to Arthur to share his recollections with us. In his late eighties, Arthur is still enjoying the challenges of working five days a week as the head engineer of his own company, employing some thirty people. Over the years, but not to bothered by the fact, Arthur had noticed that he was not mentioned in Land Rover's history. Alex's interviews triggered Arthur to share his story and revisit those days over sixty years ago.

We established a cross continental interview routine. I would provide

Alex with a few areas to explore with Arthur. Alex used his video camera to record Arthur for an hour long interview in Brisbane. The benefits of current technology enabled Alex to convert the video and download it to me overnight via Skype. Alex would usually give me a brief overview of what was said. I couldn't wait to hear what 'historic bomb shells' would come next. To make cross-referencing easier, I compiled a list of the vehicles Arthur had received, key dates, calendars and time lines from 1947. Memories are never perfect and I was a touch weary. Memory faculty depends on age, experience at the time, and what you were doing. I know my ability to recall events are never perfect when I ask others for their view of past events and information. Thankfully Julian Paton (the co-owner of 16) does extensive work and research in physiology. He provided insights on how mind recall works, in particular long term memory. From a physiological perspective, Arthur's memories were a perfect case of memory by association. The more and more Arthur spoke about those times, the better he became at recalling. More pieces of this puzzle fell into place. Many of the facts from Arthur's astounding recollections just came out and figuratively hit us in the face.

There was so much information in the first interviews. From a historical point of view it was awesome. Arthur's memory was crystal clear, and he shared points in great detail. He intrigued us with his fascination about major engineering problems and changes. The first article on Arthur Goddard appeared in *Full Grille* in the May 2009 edition. It covered a few minor myths and unanswered questions on the very early vehicles and how the Wilks brothers and the senior engineers worked together.

When writing the articles, we documented Arthur's perspective and used italics to highlight any information that required further detail. Dave Hanson thought this structure worked well, so we used it throughout. The first myth that was resolved by Arthur's recollections was the alloy bodywork made from left over World War two aircraft aluminium. No extensive scientific research had been done before on the aluminium used. A fellow Land Rover enthusiast in Melbourne, Ian Duddy has his own laboratory and scanning electron microscope. He tested samples parts to determine what materials were used for manufacturing and plating. As well as providing data to help find out what materials were used, some of the scientific terms completely bamboozled the rest of the club members. We had not yet analysed the alloy body work, and with having discovered Arthur, there was no need. Arthur straight off the mark let us know that the material was a then new aluminium alloy called Birmabright, which came in ¼ hard and ½ hard sheets that worked hardened. Julian and I knew this all ready as number 16 had identified Birmabright panel. It is possible to read the id markings in the corner of the seat panel. I was going to use this information for a later club magazine article, but the perfect opportunity was now. So in it went.

The second myth was another fortuitous discovery. The early photos of *Huey* first show her with a painted rear body section and, shortly after as the development progressed, with an unpainted one. This had always seemed odd to me, but not to Arthur. To test the off road clearance for axles and propeller shafts, the engineers cut open a section of *Huey's* bodywork. The test was done to make sure that nothing scraped or damaged the chassis or bodywork. Dave and I carefully studied some of old black and white photos that '*The Motor Magazine*' had taken of *Huey* shortly after off road testing began with the painted rear body on. Suddenly, a clearly cut away gap in the centre section of the body became obvious. Using computer software, we were able to zoom in on the rear body and use the photo in a magazine article to corroborate Arthur's memory of events.

A very early picture of *Huey* in which you can see the cut in the rear body

After the test was satisfactorily completed, the rear body was replaced with a new uncut unpainted one. It was done, no doubt, to save the engineers from getting their suits dirty! In those days, the engineers wore their business suits when they did test runs. Arthur recalls that he would never have dreamed of returning to the Rover factory offices without a suit on. In the various discussions that we had about his past career, it became clear that Arthur was certainly someone who continued looking to the future. We realised when interviewing Arthur, even though he was eighty nine, because he had such a busy and eventful career that he had never ever stopped to look back.

After being shown a number of old photographs, Arthur gave Alex a photo of himself in Edinburgh, with some colleagues about to deliver a then new Royal Review 86" Land Rover to the Queen. At this point, we were still trying to work out how and why Arthur had 'disappeared.' This photo made us further realise Arthur's significance. With a task as important as delivering a vehicle to Her Majesty The Queen, the head of Rover, would either deliver it himself or give the task to the bloke in charge of that model. As we were very familiar with the old photos, we easily recognised Arthur and knew clearly what he looked like and how he stood and dressed. It was now easy to identify him in many of the early testing photos of *Huey* with his colleague, Johnny Cullen always in the driver's seat.

The magazine was published and received a great response from all in the club. I always get a natural high out of writing and sharing new information with my mates. This time I received an email from James Taylor, the well known motoring historian and author of many Rover history books. James was just as pleased and astonished by Arthur's appearance as any of us. From what James knew it was obvious that Arthur was an unknown variable in Land Rover's history.

Alex and Russell thought this was like the ultimate Christmas and birthday and wrapped into one. They kept interviewing Arthur, and I kept writing. We were also trying to piece together the story of how Arthur had arrived on the Brisbane business estate. I was determinedly digging into the historical files at Gaydon. Using the list that I had compiled of the test vehicles that had been allocated to the development and engineering departments and to Arthur, it was easy to follow the oral history that Arthur shared. The development vehicles for the future 86" and long wheelbase variants was one area that, to date, had not been fully researched. During the early days, Rover's photographer, Toft Bate had kept a thorough record of the photographs. They were carefully dated, numbered and catalogued. Over time, many of the photographs and negatives have been lost and misplaced. Thousands of factory photographs of Series 1 Land Rovers from 1948 to 1958 had been saved and stored at Gaydon but without any clear order. Recently, many boxes of the old photos had been brought back into a more manageable order. This is thanks to Roger who sorted the photographs into various sub categories of wheelbases, station wagons, fire engines etc.

Arthur and colleagues in Edinburgh ready to hand over the Royal 86" Land Rover to the Queen

Persistence does pay off. Now that we could clearly recognise him, Arthur started appearing in many of the old pictures. Photographs of other interesting engineering prototypes also came to light. Many were in Toft Bates photo ledger and easy to date. I started writing the next set of articles with a clear time line linked to Land Rover's early development. Dates from the dispatch books, factory registrations' books and the photo ledgers helped to bring Arthur's brilliant story to life. James Taylor suggested that the P4 Rover car prototype, made from a Studebaker, called the 'Roverbaker' should be included in our next article about Arthur, as a huge amount of development work had gone into it during Arthur's time at Rover. It worked a treat.

We were determined that the second article was going to be even better than the first This was done partly by including cross referenced material. Dave is brilliant as editor. He laid out the pages with photos, and it came out extremely well. Alex's interview inspired Arthur to share his thoughts about various developments, all of which were fascinating. Arthur roared with laughter when Alex asked if he recalled a Studebaker based P4 Rover car prototype? "Oh, you mean the Roverbaker," replied Arthur. This was music to our ears. Arthur's fine sense of humour added to the stories. He was a real 'hands on' engineer. Arthur laughingly referred to himself as one of 'the dirty finger nail brigade.'

The development long wheel base Land Rover

The next topic that Arthur discussed was fixing the known front wheel wobble problem. This occurred with the development of the first long wheel base test vehicle. Changing the front leaf spring hinging shackles from leading at the front of the springs to trailing stopped the front wheel wobble that had plagued some of the early vehicles. Arthur described the engineering problems that arose due to the way the springs hinged and moved. This new design resulted in different movement of the front differential's drive flange and wear on the front propeller shaft to way it was first designed, but halted the wheel wobble problems they had. It took Dave and I three evenings to write a description of this in simple enough language for others to understand the engineering issues that Arthur and his team resolved. This discussion led Arthur to describe the development of the first long wheelbase. Not much was previously known about this development that occurred from mid to late 1949. The conversation covered the military vehicles in Europe, including the Minerva assembled Completely Knocked Down vehicles. Arthur mentioned that they managed to borrow a Mercedes Unimog from the Belgians to take back to Solihull to test. Land Rover also tested vehicles in Spain. There is photographic evidence with Gaydon housing a vast collection of photos about this.

All this talk of wheel wobble and highly detailed suspension geometry led Arthur to a story about the Motor Industry Research Association (MIRA) and the Belgian Pavé facility there. He had helped build it as part of Rover's early contribution to the facility. After this revelation, the story really came alive. The internet is a great facility to do initial research. We used it to get basic information about MIRA. To get detailed knowledge of a now top secret motor industry research facility was going to be tougher. I had an old *Country Life* article from the 1950s about MIRA and the various facilities there. The article explained the great job being done at MIRA testing cars to destruction for the post war export drive. I had got hold of it for a picture of a very early Land Rover that was tested there. I didn't know much about that Land Rover except chassis number of the vehicle and that it had been dispatched directly to MIRA for testing.

One morning, the Pavé story all fell into place when Roger Crathorne called on the phone. He had been glued to his copy of '*Full Grille*,' reading it from cover to cover. Roger wanted to talk to me about the second Goddard article. This article covered Arthur's recollections about the front spring developments and the 80" wheel wobble. In the 1970s, Roger and his team experimented with having front mounted shackles on the front axle's leaf springs. This was the design that most other 4x4 manufacturers used at the time. Roger drew the same conclusion as Arthur and left the front leaf springs on the Land Rover unchanged. Besides knowing Rover and its engineering testing inside out, Roger is also a huge early vehicle fan, having owned numerous 80" Land Rovers. While discussing the front spring developments and wheel wobble, Roger referred to the work that he had done at MIRA testing the original Range Rover prototypes. This corresponded with Arthur's story about Rover building the Belgian Pavé facility at MIRA. When Roger was doing testing at MIRA in the 1960s, no one could remember who at Rover had built the Pavé track. I mentioned Arthur's Pavé recollections. The revelation that Arthur was the missing early Land Rover engineer came to light about a minute later. I emailed the *Country Life* article to Roger who, in turn, contacted the MIRA press office. The press office sent us an old but very high resolution picture of the same early development vehicle flying over a small speed hump. This was all totally incredible. All involved were awe struck by the stories that were being uncovered. And more discoveries were yet to come.

Michael Bishop

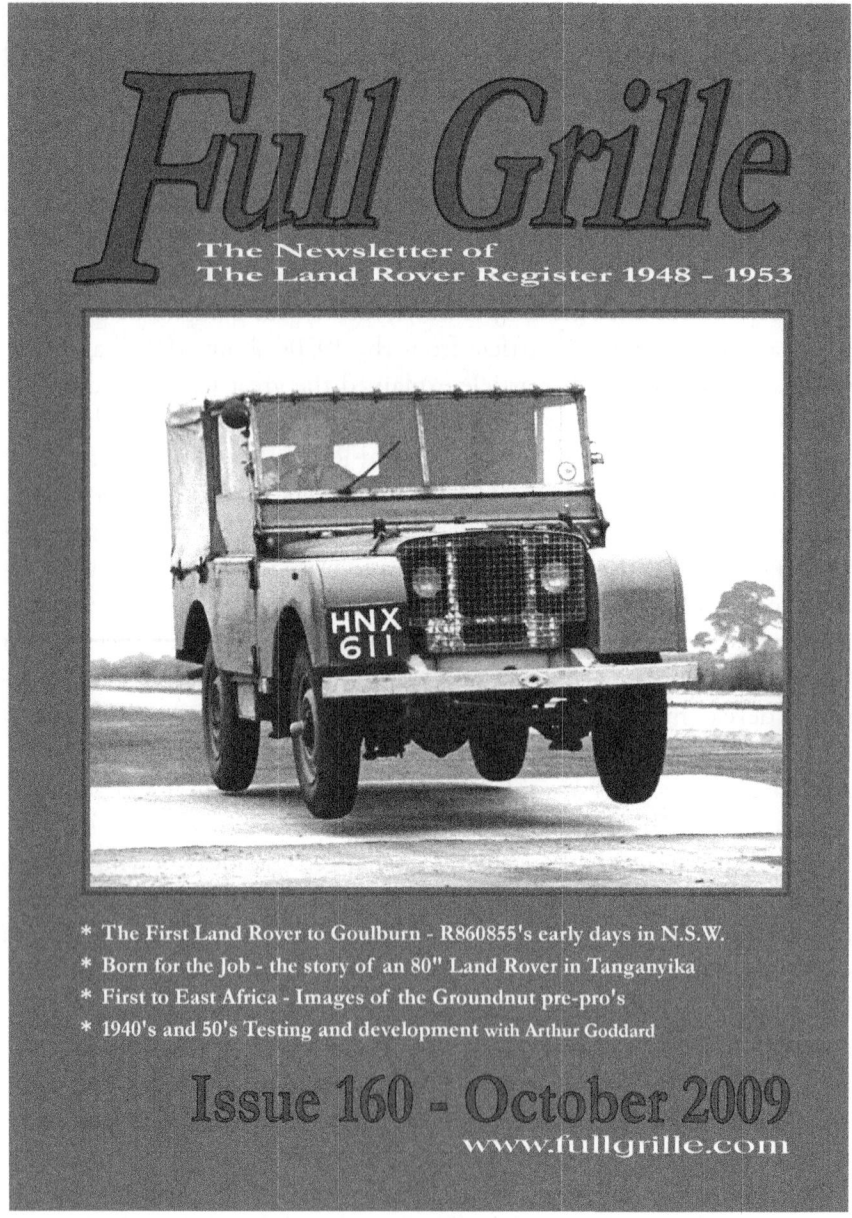

Full Grille
The Newsletter of
The Land Rover Register 1948 - 1953

* The First Land Rover to Goulburn - R860855's early days in N.S.W.
* Born for the Job - the story of an 80" Land Rover in Tanganyika
* First to East Africa - Images of the Groundnut pre-pro's
* 1940's and 50's Testing and development with Arthur Goddard

Issue 160 - October 2009
www.fullgrille.com

Cover of 'Full Grille' 160 with the 1948 MIRA test vehicle flying over a speed hump

From *1940's and 50's Developments and Testing with Arthur Goddard. Full Grille 160 October 2009*

When it came to the Land Rover, Arthur and the initial Land Rover project team had made there own test track over the air raid shelters at the

Lode Lane factory but Arthur says to really simulate properly you have to have the vehicles go over the same section of road day in and out and know that the weather conditions that may have changed won't change the out come of the tests as you didn't know if the muddy puddle was deeper this time than last time so you couldn't tell if a test then was more severe now or previously. He said the tests at MIRA were all marked so you could set up everything to be exactly the same for each test. Arthur tells us Rover just after the war had been involved in the initiative to set up MIRA research facility in around 1946 and Rover's part was to make a test section of road that could really test out durability of suspension systems of the vehicles for places with very harsh roads. Arthur says the Motor Industry banded together and an old aerodrome was purchased just outside Nuneaton at Lindley in Leicestershire.

The idea with MIRA was to make test tracks and roads for testing to simulate over seas conditions with corrugations, water splashes, dust and all kind of things that vehicles may encounter outside the UK. All of the manufacturers involved made a contribution to the tracks being made and Rover's part was to make a section called the 'Belgian Pavé'

Arthur says he and Bro Ward, went to Brussels and found a section of Pavé on the outskirts just towards the start of the then new Jabbeke Highway that was exceptionally rough and uneven. These bad sections of road where known to have destroyed vehicles suspension often in as little as six months, so replicating this road at MIRA would be of great use to the Engineers testing for export. That got themselves levels and plans to, record and measured the unevenness and the size of the rocks and took pictures. Once back they laid out a copy of the Pavé at MIRA with similar stones set in concrete around the MIRA course and it was about 1 mile long. Arthur says that the Pavé was specifically made with testing the Land Rover in mind and was put in about mid 1949. Rover engineers tested all there vehicles on the various tracks that MIRA had to offer but the Land Rover spent much of its test time on the Pavé and another section called the Wavy road. Arthur says starting off with these they had to decide what was a reasonable test. So they tried various distances say 500 miles on the Pavé and see how the vehicles would survive. If it did 500 miles on the test then they would go to 700 and by this point if something broke, it wasn't good and needed re designing or strengthening.

Arthurs says they ultimately set an aim that all Rover's vehicles had to be able to do 1000 miles on the Pavé as it it put so much stress through the whole vehicle and bodywork and anything that wasn't strong enough broke. Arthur also added that on the Pavé testing shock absorbers were difficult and you always had to make compromises. He says the telescopic type even though cheap and easy to fit, he feels that they are in many ways a bad design as on the tests they got very hot and for the Land Rover's they didn't want to allow them to cool so they had to install cooling fans to stop the Shock absorber bushes from catching on fire. He also says that finding a shock absorber that would do a 1000 mile on the Pavé wasn't necessarily the right one. This may just have meant that this type isn't working hard enough and not controlling the vehicle. So one that lasts 800 miles may be the best compromise to ride where obviously one that lasted only 300 miles was clearly no good. Arthur thinks really that for this kind of work the earlier in vehicle history 'pre war' chassis mounted lever arm type automotive shock absorbers would have been a better answer to off road and rough ground type of use as the problem of dispersing the heat was less as it could run though the chassis where the rubber mounted telescopic type you had very little to play with to get rid of the heat other than the size of the unit. The telescopic type were just so cost affective for production so that's the way it had to be.

It was an incredible feeling to add all this totally new information to the greater Land Rover story. We came across another vehicle that looked like a very interesting prototype that we had seen in some Land Rover books. It was a very early vehicle that had been fitted with a Rolls Royce B.40 engine. The engine was for the, then up and coming, specialist military vehicle and now Land Rover competitor, the Austin Champ. Ultimately thirty three more of these vehicles with B.40 Rolls engines were built with input from the MOD. The early vehicle was sent to Arthur for testing. The story of having tested a competitor's vehicle's engine in the Land Rover was not only unusual and to date unheard of and also too interesting to ignore.

Arthur fully shared his knowledge with us about Rover and Rolls Royce during the war. For better or worse, Alex and Russell had a crash course on Land Rover and Rover, the company. Our enthusiasm coupled with what we knew encouraged Arthur and often the conversations covered the unexpected. Arthur was initially deeply involved with Rover's wartime engine developments for Rolls Royce's Merlin engines use in tanks. This project had come to Rover as part of a swap when Rolls Royce took over the Jet engine development from Rover. The end of this stage was part of Arthur's first days at Rover in the mid 1940s. Lucas aerospace worked very closely on the Whittle Jet engine project with Rover and then Rolls Royce too. Arthur was part also of the team that helped developed the Rover Jet cars, along with his brother Les, who worked for Lucas aerospace on jet engines and Rovers gas turbine engine. In his inimical style, Arthur eagerly told the story of the Jet engine, and Rover's involvement in the development. It seems that the development was somewhat controversial. Frank Whittle invented that jet engine. The British Government provided funding for the engine's development and required that Frank work with Rover. From reading between the lines on what has been written to date, it is possible to sense the personality clashes, controversy and the pressure put on engineering developments to support the war effort. During my meeting with Spen King, I sensitively raised the subject. Spen's interpretation of personalities and events was very similar to Arthur's. Rover had a man who took the Jet engine and ran with it. "The Gloucester Meteor in the end was powered by our (Rover's) engine didn't please Whittle too much." Yet again, discussions, more digging and another few revelations surfaced. This all provided further material for the next *Full Grille*.

Rover and Rolls Royce

One of the other vehicles I have been curious for Arthur to tell us about was the Land Rover's fitted with the B 40 engine. Having read about the various reasons why a special 33 were converted by Hudson Motor's but have there own parts book and manual and also many believe that there was a Development B40 Land Rover made from an earlier vehicle that the 33 British Military examples that were converted. Another trawl through the Dispatch book gives us

R862561, dispatched 'In' 11/02/49 and 'Out' 15/03/49 To Mr Goddard, Rover Co, then 30/08/49 to FVDE Cobham. Rolls Royce Engine.

So Arthur says he still doesn't fully understand why they had to do this project, but someone had decided in the idea to make a 'British Jeep' after the war and that Austin ultimately made it would be a good idea to use the B40 and for a spares supply having it related to the 6 cylinder and 8 cylinder version. Yes the idea had some merit for spare parts to have almost identical engines but Rolls Royce was basically an Aircraft company that happened to make cars to that kind of tolerance and this made their products like their engines really expensive. The B40 engine was somewhere around twice the price of a Land Rover. At Rover they felt there own design and engine was more than capable of what was really needed by the military. He says the B40 engine wasn't to difficult to get into the engine bay of the Land Rover and the vehicle went off to have to be tested and they didn't really have to think about it too much after that as it was the military's project.

So whilst on the topic of Rolls Royce we commented that Rover and Rolls appeared to be very close at this time just after the war, having shared the Jet engine development during the war and the Meteor tank engine Rover made *from the Rolls Royce Merlin engine, W A Robotham had one of the very first pre production Land Rover's etc etc. Arthur says Rover and Rolls Royce were very very close. Both companies also with Lucas as well and they had been close since war technically but also socially at the upper management level. They had all become very close as when Frank Whittle first came to Rover with his Jet engine and famously didn't agree what was being done at Rover. Arthur says one of the reasons for this was a Rover man in the Drawing Office by the name of Adrian Lombard was working with Whittle engine and made his own developments to the design and it worked much better allowing the jet engine to breathe and hence work properly. Lombard's designed Rover's W.B2/26 jet engine which became the Rolls Royce Derwent Jet Engine. Arthur says this was just before his time but his brother worked as an Engineer in the Lucas aero section, which were also closely involved and after the war they had both knew closely many involved in this story. The compressor blades for the jet were similar in many ways to the super changers that Rolls Royce made and it became obvious that Rolls with there aero expertise should take over the project. Rover's man Lombard ultimately became Roll Royce Chief Engineer - Director of Engineering of the Aero Engine Division by the 1950's and Rover was very proud of this fact.*

Not knowing much about jet engine developments or Frank Whittle, we did not have any background or context for the information that Arthur had shared with us. After trawling through the old *'Flight'* magazine articles, I was startled by what can be found as well as what hadn't been brought to light yet. Lombard's story was there, hidden away with information about him that is not in widely known. Due to his jet engine expertise, he had a very successful career at Rolls Royce Jet engines, though unfortunately he died at his desk in the late 1960s. Another brilliant, yet forgotten, Rover man. Arthur summed up the whole Frank Whittle/Rover/ Rolls-Royce episode as only he can.

'You see, the trouble Frank had at Rover is that he was a very bright youngster with a very good idea. But in those days you went to a huge engineering company like Rover and then you find suddenly you're in a place with 500 or so other very bright youngsters and unfortunately more often than not there is one brighter than you. That's what happened to Frank and he didn't like it'

It felt as though the story had gone way off the mark and we had taken a few steps too far. Telling the full story, though, seemed the right thing to do. Recounting the story did not generate any negative feedback, but it did generate more curiosity - did anyone know of a book about Adrian Lombard? The query came from member of the Wilks family. It was interesting that they were the source of the request. James Taylor, editor of *Land Rover Enthusiast Magazine,* sent his Australian correspondent to interview Arthur. We recorded the interview on video. Arthur was at his vintage best with a story about secretly visiting a mate at Harry Ferguson's tractor factory at Standard in Coventry to see how the gear ratios are set for ploughing. We recorded Arthur talking about the Rover 'freewheel' transfer box and more steering geometry care of Mr Akerman and his steering principals. This recording was used as a teaser video on The Register's Youtube Channel to share Arthur and his stories with enthusiasts across the world.

We started planning a "welcome home visit" for Arthur that corresponded with a trip that he was making to England in late April 2010. Roger and the public relations team at Land Rover were assisting in every capacity. For the next article, we covered the internal workings at Rover and the unreleased M Type car that Rover worked on prior to the Land Rover. The article also included Arthur's story of a secret visit to Standard in Coventry in 1947 to find out how Standard determined the ratios needed for the new Standard engine in the Ferguson tractor. We also proudly shared that we were going to be fortunate enough to have Arthur back in England in May 2010. We advised club members to get in quick and put their name down for his gala dinner event. One of the first replies came back from one of Spencer Wilks sons. We were now getting somewhere with the Arthur Goddard story, with more pieces of the greater puzzle appearing by the day. Arthur too was beginning to genuinely enjoy the story coming to light. From his point of view, he had always wondered why know one had been in touch!

Michael Bishop

Arthur's official photo at Rover as found in the archives

The Factory Plans

In anticipation of Arthur's return visit 'home' to Solihull, this was a bumper edition of *Full Grille*. It was really all happening. Land Rover were planning to honour Arthur with a two day visit. Roger researched through old files to find more information about Arthur and the work that Rover undertook in the 1940s and 1950s. Arthur's old work passport photo was the first item to come about. Next was a drawing of the rear section of a 104" Land Rover chassis. It was not the usual long wheelbase 107" or later 109" unit. There was a drawing of an American styled four door Land Rover 'Station Car' built by coach builders Mulliners of Birmingham for us to discuss with Arthur. As luck would have it, I had stumbled across the vehicle in the old Rover dispatch books and its registration number too. Arthur believes this all contributed to a greater project that related to the Road Rover and regular Land Rover Station Wagons. It was part of the process of trying to decide which path the Station Wagon should take, whether it would be based on the Road Rover or something more like the Land Rover.

Michael Bishop

August 1954. The 100,000th Land Rover with Arthur on the left again

It took a bit more effort to understand the 104" chassis, as it was one of the few things Arthur couldn't recall directly what it was. He knew the first prototype long wheelbase wasn't a 107" but wasn't sure exactly what it was. We discovered the answer when he described the lengthening the wheelbase from the 80" to 86". We used that information for the fourth *Full Grille* article.

From *'Full Grille' 161 December 09*

The early days learning from the 80" were invaluable in making the 86" as good as complete as it is. I commented how the 86" is really a clever layout in using the same length prop shaft at the front and rear. To which Arthur said that we managed to achieve the aims of that project and keep parts supply simple with out any added cost of an extra part that was needed which is always a strong consideration. He went on to describe exactly the extra 6" length wheelbase and the 9"more over hang they could gain meant a 25% increase in load space.

And further to role that the 104" played in the 80/86" equation and how it became the 107".

From *'Full Grille' 162 Feburary 10*

How the 86" fits in with all this is in making the 86" the engineers extended the rear road springs by six" which given that the axle is in the middle

of the spring meant that lined up along side one another the 86" axle is an extra 3" behind the spring pins than an 80". 104" + 3" makes 107". Easy. The original LWB design was 104" but became 107" when you add the longer rear spring of an 86". So back to the 104" it makes perfect sense. Add two feet (24") to the 80" and another 50% for the overhang as Arthur says with the 86" and you get 3 feet or nearly double the load space of an 80"

We compared the 104" and Land Rover Station Car by overlaying the chassis drawings from the workshop manuals. This proved the points that Arthur made. Dave and Alex made smart looking copies for the magazine article. These copies looked spectacular and added the wow factor to this edition of the magazine.

Spen had said the history books don't or maybe can't "touch the sides on the reality". This was becoming quite apparent. Although the Land Rover history had been well documented with words and pictures, many of the dynamics and much of excitement of the early years had been missed or passed over. This meant that a multi-dimensional story had to date only shown one or two of its dimensions. By now, as a consequence of the interviews, Arthur had been reflecting upon Land Rover of the 1950s for many months. One of the best anecdotes was that Arthur and Cullen had driven a welder model and standard Land Rover to the 1948 Amsterdam Motor show despite him saying he had nothing to do with the marketing department! The Amsterdam Motor Show proved to be one of the iconic marketing opportunities for Land Rover. It was a seminal experience for the engineers and for Land Rover. Not only were Land Rovers still being tested and a special licence to drive the prototypes was required, but also they were the engineers to do it. Arthur and Cullen were the technical experts on Rover's stand. This was the 30th of April launch show and as the Land Rover was still in development, the sales team hadn't been fully briefed on the full technical detail. Only Cullen and Goddard could answer those questions. It was Arthur's first trip abroad, and was one to remember. Arthur stayed at the Doelen Hotel in Amsterdam along with his friend Bob Swann, the Chief Engineer at Lincoln Electric. Lincoln manufactured the welding units for the vehicle kits and would be contracted to supply the huge welding machines for welding together the now famous Land Rover box sectioned chassis rails. Bob Swann enjoyed life too. They started the evening with martinis at the bar. From what I knew now, this was Arthur's style.

The Land Rover was already a hit, as the military were very keen to order over 1000 vehicles. Over the years, enthusiasts had tried to find out further details about Land Rover at the 1948 Amsterdam Motor show. Up to 1998 only two pieces of information surfaced, one was factual, the other proved not. These pieces of information were 1) photos of the welder Land Rover on the stand and 2) a story that a Land Rover had some trouble with the clutch or gear selection. The vehicle outside the main hall supposedly had problems with all sorts of gearbox related crunching and grinding noises. We shared this with Arthur. He is certain that nothing was wrong or went wrong. If a problem, as serious as that, had arisen at a highly respected show to introduce a brand new vehicle there would have been in Arthur's words "hell to pay" back at the factory. It seems that the gearbox story may be something else. Could be just confusion in how the 'prototype' transmission levers worked.

The fifth article on Arthur Goddard also covered testing the independent front suspension systems for the 86" Land Rover. I called Arthur to ask about a few very detailed points, and this time he had a question for us. Arthur was interested to know about what had happened to his replacement, Colonel Jack Pogmore at Rover. Arthur recalled that after he left and went to Girling as technical director that Rover split the assistant chief engineer job in two, with separate assistant chief engineers for cars and Land Rovers. Pogmore had come from the Ministry of Defence and had been in vehicle procurement. Arthur had not thought about this before, but was now a bit curious. Arthur shared that apart from Alex and I, Jack Pogmore was the only other person who had ever been in touch about the Land Rover. This contact was made years ago, in the days soon after Arthur left Rover. Jack was often in touch asking detailed engineering questions. Arthur felt that our questions were in the same vein as Jack's, only fifty years later.

I contacted Roger to see if he could help answer Arthur's question. "Arthur wants to know what happened to Pogmore," I told Roger. So far, the focus of the research had been on the early vehicles, not later staff changes. Roger shared that Pogmore left Rover soon after Roger had started his apprenticeship in 1962. As a result, Roger did not know much about him. Roger's lack of familiarity on this did not prove to be a problem. I contacted Roger's early Range Rover engineering team colleague, Geof Miller. Geof had joined Rover just after Arthur had left. After Arthur left, Tom Barton was caretaking the Land Rover assistant chief engineer role and expected that he would be offered the job. Tom had initially worked in the drawing office for Gordon Bashford for many years, and had a lot of engineering experience. It was not to be. Jack Pogmore came in from outside of Rover and got the job. At the time, Tom was disappointed that he did not get the role. Geof felt that Jack was a typical military style 'man manager type' – a very nice chap, but was not a real engineer like Arthur.

Arthur would be a hard act to follow for anyone, and I could get the picture of what was going on. Roger had recently given me a compact disc containing old factory drawings to help us confirm Arthur's recollections. Like myself, Alex and Arthur these drawings came from Australia too!!. The old Rover Australia CKD plants had full factory drawings from 1947 to manufacture their own parts and one of Roger's Australian colleagues had sent them over. It also showed that plans for the Series 2, or Mark 2 Land Rover as it was first called, were well underway by the end of 1955. Arthur leaving Rover gave the company the chance to have a military man in place that knew what the main customer wanted. Geof fondly remembers that Jack was very keen for everyone, especially the younger engineers, to get the right qualifications. As a result, Geof, along with many other young engineers attended college and obtained a formal engineering qualification. He will be forever thankful to Jack for that.

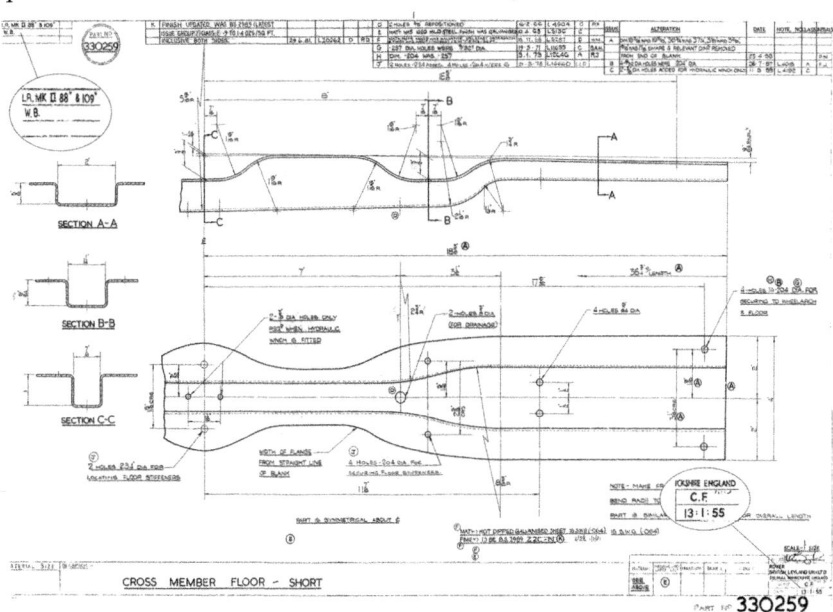

A drawing from early 1955 of a Land Rover Mark 2 bodywork part. The Mark 2 became known as the Series 2 a little later on

Pogmore remained Land Rover's assistant chief engineer for a number of years and eventually focussed most of his time on engineering administration. Tom Barton, then, got the job that he had been missed out on before. Not long after, Jack left Rover. Despite not knowing the exact details, this all seemed feel somewhat uneasy. It was the 1960s and the British motor industry was just about to embark on some really difficult days. Having found out what I could, I called Arthur and shared what had happened to Jack. The information that I shared satisfied Arthur's curiosity. Nonetheless, I couldn't help but wonder how the Land Rover would have evolved had Arthur stayed at Rover or if he had even wondered that himself. When Arthur left Rover, the Series 2 plans were all set ready to go.

It was getting close to a year since Arthur had appeared. The group of us involved in telling his story had managed to turn the early history of Land Rover on its head. Planning was well underway for the 'An evening with Arthur Goddard' event, hosted by the Land Rover Register 1948 to 1953 and the Land Rover Series 1 clubs. The clubs did not have prior experience of organising an event like this for Land Rover collectors and enthusiasts. We knew that a nice comfortable hotel with great food, wine and hospitality was Arthur's kind of place. For some time, Roger and I had been trying to agree dates for the event. Arthur was happy to take part. He had two constraints. One was that the date did not conflict with school holidays. The other was that he had to be back in Australia in June for business. Given the opportunity to choose the day, I looked through the calendar and dates from the old dispatch books and ledgers from the late 40s and early 50s. I was very familiar with the dispatch books and ledgers, as I had used them before to link events and key dates with work days and weekends. Using modern technology, this correlation is very easy to do and suddenly I noticed something slightly incredible.

Apart from the first two months of 2010, the 1948 calendar year is the same as 2010 to the day. This meant we could have Arthur back at Solihull on Friday 30th of April. This was to the day sixty two years after the launch at Amsterdam! With all that had happened so far, it would have been mad to choose any other day. I booked Solihull for this historic date. The plan was for Arthur to arrive at Heathrow on April 27th. Arthur was confident that he would not have Jetlag and it would be just in time for the 30 April events. The plan was cast in stone.

The Ash Cloud nerves

With all and sundry looking forward to Arthur's arrival, *An evening with Arthur Goddard"* was arranged to be held at The Chesford Grange Hotel near Kenilworth in Warwickshire. After their Coventry factory was bombed in the Second World War, Rover used Chesford Grange as an office and started work on the jet engine design there. We thought it was a nice touch to have the historic link to Rover and to Arthur's wartime aero work. Chesford Grange is also near Maurice Wilks' home during that time, Blackdown Manor. Everything had gone so incredibly well and then the Eyjafjallajöekull volcano erupted in Iceland. The only worry we had through this whole adventure was this darn volcano. It first erupted on 14 April 2010. From the 15th through the 20th of April, the eruption entered a second phase and created an ash cloud that led to the closure of most of Europe's airspace. Many flights within, to, and from Europe were cancelled. It reputedly created the highest level of air travel disruption since the War.

I dug deep and kept quiet as the mass media started blanketing us with all the bad news that the volcanic ash had caused. Newspapers, radio and television were full of sad and sorry stories about people stuck here and there. The news reported that it was going to take months to sort out the backlog of flights. Their overt message was to forget any plans you may have had. Given how fortunate we had been so far in discovering this story, I felt that even this wasn't going to be able to disrupt our plans. And, thankfully, it didn't. Alex; however, almost "missed the boat". He had decided to get a UK working visa and take the opportunity to live, learn and travel abroad As a result, he had been in England since before Christmas 2009.

The end of the Land Rover Production line at Solihull today

The plan was for Alex to return to Australia to see his family and then to travel back to the UK with Arthur. At the time of the volcanic eruption, Alex was with his family in Brisbane and due to travel to the UK. Eventually, the ash cloud cleared over the UK and their flight was one of the first confirmed safe entry into the Heathrow. Alex, however, had a slightly different ticket. Though far less expensive than a standard ticket, it works on the basis of the ticket holder getting the next available seat. Due to flight disruptions, there were no "next available seats" and his ticket was cancelled. Arthur, who had a standard ticket, flew without Alex and duly arrived at Heathrow at the scheduled time. I was there to pick him up. It was great to finally meet him in person. Jaguar Land Rover had lent Arthur a new Freelander to use for the duration of his stay. It was a Baltic Blue HSE model with all the options and Almond Windsor leather interior. A great car and Arthur and I both loved its comfort.

Building luxury cars may not have been his favourite job at times, but that does not stop Arthur Goddard from using and enjoying them. I had asked Roger if we could borrow a Discovery because one can film out the back of it very easily. Due to the high sales demand, none were available. We had noticed this. Julian and I had kept our Pre Production 16 at a local dealer as part of a historic display. They were always awaiting a consignment of new Land Rovers that had not yet arrived and were grateful to have old Number 16 on display. Otherwise the showroom would have

They Found Our Engineer

looked a touch sparse. The demand for Land Rovers was sky high and, every Land Rover in production was already sold. A snowy winter in the UK certainly does good marketing for Land Rovers, despite any global financial crisis.

The idea to film out the back of a new Discovery arose from a press release the Series One Club used to publicise Arthur's visit. As a consequence, ITV central news got in touch. This lead to Teeafit Sound and Vision, a television and video production company, wanting to produce a documentary about Arthur's visit. Our response was "Great, the more, the merrier."

Alex eventually made it back to England. He was just in time to take part in the Arthur Goddard events, as the ash cloud continued to cause major travel disruptions. Young and determined, he didn't give up easily. From Brisbane he flew to Sydney. He changed his ticket to fly from Sydney to San Francisco. In San Francisco, he used his frequent flyer points to board a British Always flight to London. Alex arrived in London on the 28th of April, just one day before we took Arthur Godard to his first interview with researchers at the British Motor Industry Heritage Trust at Gaydon.

Arthur outside the Solihull Land Rover factory with current Solihull Manufacturing director Alan Volkaerts

Arthur's visit consisted of two weeks of Land Rover-ing. It was a huge success. We recorded a video entitled 'Stop Gap' that told Arthur's story. Assured of an action packed event, Land Rover invited journalists from *Land Rover Owner, Classic and Sports Car Magazine* and *Land Rover Monthly Magazine* as guests to the factory day on the 30th of April. Arthur took it all in his stride. Roger, Dave and I had worked hard to find the original locations where a number of photographs had been taken of Arthur sixty years ago. With Arthur, we revisited many of the sites. Arthur knew them all, as well as every good pub across the Midlands from Solihull to Silverstone. These were the places where all the top car engineers went and dined between testing of course!

Since moving to Australia, Arthur made regular visits to England every few year to visit his elder son Stewart, other members of the family and friends too. In many ways, it was as if he had never left. Land Rover put on a great day. We were taken on tour of the Solihull plant. We visited the old offices and meeting rooms, the current Defender and Range Rover production lines and the Defender body shop, where the body panels are assembled in exactly the same way as they always have. The head of each area was poised to meet the guest of honour, and the motoring press following him like bees. Arthur was in his element and fully enjoyed the tour of his old workplace, especially the engineering sections.

Arthur inspecting new Defender bulkheads with Graham Silvers, Mark Saville and Roger Crathorne

Classic and Sports Car journalist, Richard Bremner obtained a vintage

They Found Our Engineer

Arthur Goddard quote – "I didn't have a lot of sympathy for the arts and crafts side. I'm a cold blooded Engineer." Bremner included the quote in his article on Arthur's visit. All were most taken by seeing the vast press that made the panels for the current Range Rover, Discovery and Range Rover Sport - a breathtaking piece of modern engineering. Arthur admired an anti sway bar design on the current Defender. He felt that it would be a great design to adapt for his off road trailer suspension. He then went on to talk to the engineers about it. Along with all the current Land Rovers, we had a small collection of Series 1 vehicles on hand for Arthur to see. Philip Bashall from the Dunsfold Land Rover Collection brought along their replica centre steer prototype. As we did not want to influence his judgement, we did not tell Arthur that replicas of the centre steer had been made.

The myth about the 'Centre Steer' and the vague details about the 'missing link' period fuelled speculation about what had happen to the original Centre Steer vehicle. Questions were always being asked. Was their one or were there many Centre Steers? Was the original Centre Steer still in existence in a barn somewhere? Tales and tall stories had been floating about for decades about the vehicle's whereabouts. Some would swear they knew where it really was today. Or that their cousin's brother-in-law knew the bloke who broke it up and had taken all the parts home with him. Or that it had been exported to Australia, New Zealand, and who knows where else. All the mystery surrounding it had made sure that it had been put on a pedestal. Roger and his team used powerful computers in the current Land Rover design department to enlarge and enhance the images. They were able to prove that despite any small differences that all the old photos were of the same Centre Steer vehicle. But what did Arthur think?

Arthur was somewhat bemused and initially surprised by the replica centre steer. It was a vehicle that he did not have much to do with on a design level. Nonetheless, he pointed out how difficult it was to use, as your legs straddled the transmission and gear lever area. As a consequence of trying to fit all the mechanical components under the bonnet, the steering box would need to occupy the same space as the back of the engine. Arthur considered that the only way it could be done was with an east west engine layout and they "didn't have that available to us." To get around this problem, the Centre Steer and its replicas use a cut down steering column in the middle of the vehicle. This steering column is connected by a huge chain to the shortened column of a left hand drive Jeep steering box, which is far from ideal. As the journalists quizzed him more and more on this design, he shared that the Engineering team back in 1947 had thought about using the central steering for about five minutes as it simply wasn't practical. Clearly the vehicle must have been just one of Maurice Wilks' pet projects' to see if his ideas were feasible.

The replica Centre Steer and early vehicle display with Arthur looking on at Land Rover Experience, Solihull

After lunch, we all went down to the nearby Packington Estate. The current Lord Aylesford owns the estate. His family has been great friends and fans of Rover and Land Rover over the years. They kindly gave us access to and let us use the property for Arthur's visit. A former quarry in the estate and a ford on the river Blyth were both used to conduct tests of the early Land Rovers. Many old test photos were taken here of *Huey* with Cullen and Goddard and a few of the original Centre Steer, as well. Lord Aylesford and his associates were able to enjoy the fun too.

We drove through the ford to take a modern day picture of us driving Arthur through the Blyth River in number 16. The ford is quite long and that day about three feet deep. These older vehicles really don't like getting wet. As the vehicle pushes the water out of the way, a bow wave rises at the front of the vehicle. If the vehicle goes a bit too much over walking pace, the wave rises too far. The wave continues over the front axle and rises further. The water gets thrown around the cooling fan and old vehicles don't have a viscous clutch to stop it. The water splashes around the engine

They Found Our Engineer

bay drowning the ignition system and spark plugs. The vehicle coughs and splutters and just stops in the middle of the river. It is possible to do some preparatory work to stop the fan working. As there was a possibility of a large number of photo takes, I didn't want to run the risk of overheating Number 16 because I had stopped the cooling system. We had a number of modern Land Rovers and tow ropes on hand. So it wasn't a huge issue if the vehicle did stop in the middle of the ford and in we went. We managed 10 crossings. Arthur had a ball chatting away in the passenger seat about past events. He also was at ease chatting with the assembled audience on hand.

Philip Bashall had a ball driving the centre steer replica back and forth through the ford. He strategically placed black cardboard to stop the ignition getting wet. As the vehicle was stone cold off the trailer, it wasn't going to be a problem for a quick few runs. In contrast, 16 was already at full operating temperature. Shortcuts and tricks could backfire badly with boiling radiators and engines. In contrast,16 got very wet. When the bow wave began to get just too high, we heard a faint ting, ting, ting, noise as the fan blades connected with the water. She only started missing a cylinder or two on the last run and then we were out. A good dose of WD40 dispersed the water, but the underside of the bonnet was soaked.

ARTHUR GODDARD IN A PRE-PRODUCTION LAND ROVER FROM 1948 BEING DRIVEN THROUGH PACKINGTON FORD - AN ORIGINAL TEST ROUTE USED BY ROVER ENGINEERS.

The official photo of Arthur and I driving 16 through the Blyth at Packington

Michael Bishop

It had been one great day. We said our good byes at the river. Arthur was keen for a beer and a chat at one of his 'locals.' It had been a long day for most, so the others all went their own way, Arthur wanted us to go to the 'Ye Old Saracen's Head' in Balsall Common a few miles down the road. Arthur was delighted by the day and was ready for some more fun. Alex chauffeured Arthur in his new-ish Defender. I made my way in the slightly grumpy 16, who slowly coughed and spluttered her way to the pub despite having been wiped down the engine bay to get rid of excess water. I had taken so long to get to the pub, that Arthur and Alex were wondering where I had been.

Arthur laughed when I entered the pub. "So you got a bit wet no doubt." Photos from 1948 captured Arthur and Johnny Cullen in *'Huey'* flying through the Blyth River with huge water splashes. Arthur admitted they had removed the fan for the photographs. Their objective was to find the optimal speed to cross the ford taking into account the bow wave height and front axle height. They found that the optimal speed was about 9 mph. Arthur continued with further background about testing Land Rovers driving in water this early one before the vehicles official launch. The water testing programme was for the military. The military knew of the Land Rover and were keen to test them. "Farmers aren't going to drive through water like that everyday," Arthur said. In contrast, military landing craft needed to be able to drive in and into deep water.

Goddard and Cullen testing *Huey* at speed through water in 1948

The engineers also went to Maurice Wilks' place on Anglesey to test how the Land Rover fared on the beach and sand dunes. These tests were needed to make sure the Land Rover was able to do the kind of testing that the military wanted. The engineers removed the bonnet to see how the water rose. The water would bounce up off the front axle straight into the fan blades and consequently kill the ignition system on the petrol engine. Arthur and Cullen realised straight away the need for a diesel engine. Diesel engines work by compression ignition. The diesel fuel is compressed so much that the fuel ignites due to the heat generated from the high compression ratio. Diesel engines, in contrast to petrol ones, don't need an electrical ignition system. But Rover didn't have one then. Arthur recalls that that engine man, Jack Swaine was put straight on the case to see what could be done, but it was going to take a while.

An Evening with Arthur Goddard

Club members and enthusiasts attended the "Evening with Arthur Goddard" and were treated to additional historic Land Rovers and resources. Current owners brought a few of Arthur's old test vehicles to the event. We had on a display a number of early Land Rover drawings that confirmed Arthur's recollections of how it all happened. The only vehicle of Arthur's that I couldn't find at the time was Prototype 86" number 1 or P86/1 from around late 1950. It had appeared in the 1990s but fallen off the radar. I had one of my hunches, a bit like the story of '260AC,' that this vehicle and Arthur had a story to tell but it wasn't to be for the moment.

Enthusiasts chat to Arthur as he looks as he inspects the line up

They Found Our Engineer

The presentation was a hit. For those who missed out, we compiled an article that appeared in *'Full Grille'* as the final part of the Arthur Goddard story.

The Factory Drawings From 'Full Grille' 164 August 2010

The 100,000th Land Rover from August 1954. Spot Arthur standing on the left hand side beside the driver. Until recently those in the photo would all have gone un-noticed and unknown; now we know that one is the man who headed up the original Land Rover project team. Same with the real story of how the Land Rover was designed and developed. But so much fascinating and curious information has all recently come to the surface and regimentally fallen into its rightful place in Land Rovers history thanks to Arthur. The evening dinner presentation was the event for those who wished to get the chance to meet and hear a bit from Arthur the opportunity to do so. The plan was to make it an easy going evening with Arthur having a chat to all about what he wanted to say. As well as the engineering side of things a few good laughs from amusing stories that had occurred from time to time at Rover. Throw in Graeme Aldous and his TV cameras recording Arthurs visit and that made it certainly something different for all involved. Graeme's DVD of Arthur's entire visit will be coming soon for those who couldn't make it.

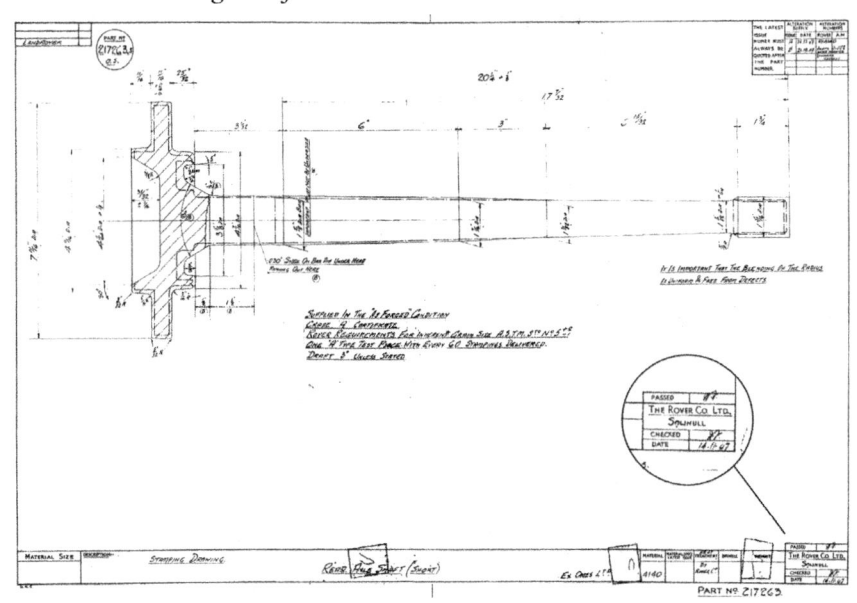

29 Land Rover rear axle shaft 217263 from the 14/11/1947

With AG the star of the show, my side was to present to the enthusiasts what factual info we had managed to find to help collaborate much of what Arthur has told us, and in reality what the Engineering team were working

Michael Bishop

on and from what Arthur had said often well ahead of what many of us had previously thought time wise.

I was able to do this mostly with the help of a number of the brilliant old Engineering drawings from Land Rover, of various parts early parts and often with dates the drawings were made on. But my plan wasn't just simply to show them but to put these new dates into context of the dates that we already knew a lot about. Such as when the Centre Steer was about and being photographed what was going on internally? When they were about to leave for the Amsterdam Motor Show how far were the team really into thinking about mass production?

The Rover Photo Ledger of Toft Bate, Rover's photographer does give us a great insight of what was going on with many areas but the very early facts of when were they designing the real Land Rover has been a touch scarce.

We know from the ledger that the Centre Steer vehicle was first photographed on the 23/09/47 and closely there after and that most of the pics used in the first broacher were taken between the 15/10/47 and the 05/11/47 which are mostly the farming shots and the others of the vehicle going through the ford were taken were taken between the 23/01/48 and the 28/01/48.

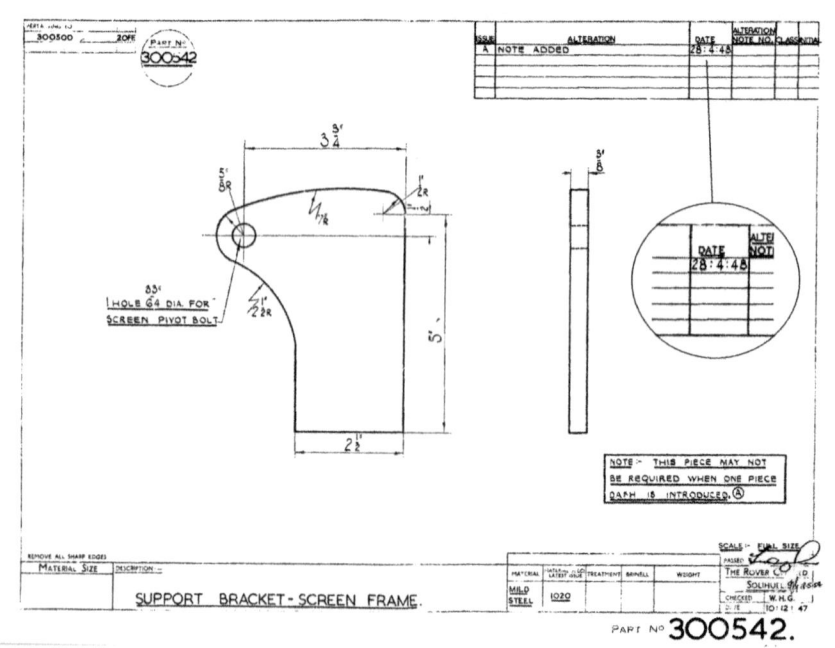

Parts 300514 and 300515 the Left and Right outer wing panels from 02/12/1947

So what were the engineers really working on at this point? As Arthur says

They Found Our Engineer

he thought about using that Centre Steer layout for 'about 5 minutes'. Well the earliest Production Part drawing we have at the moment is a drawing of the Short Rear Axle shaft, Part No 217263 which dates from 14/11/47. The second earliest Production Part so far 300514 and 300515 Right and Left Hand Outer wing panels from 02/12/47. The material is listed as Birmabright 2 Half Hard. Just as the man says!!! Certainly the Centre Steers days were quickly on the way out by the start of December 1947 and the pictures we know of it are just for publicity purpose. We had mostly realised that many are static of it ploughing and the Capstan Winch is a 'dummy unit'.

So further on we know from the dispatch dates that R01 was dispatched in on 13/03/48 and then photographed on the 14/03/48 and then extensively tested. We know the engineers cut open the bodywork to check clearances and then replaced the rear body. These photos are most taken by magazines such as 'The Motor' for the late April release of the Land Rover rather than Toft Bate. The next Land Rover photos in the ledger are of Welder, L05 on the 21/04/48, all ready to head off to Amsterdam and a week before she was 'dispatched in'

So how far down the track were the engineers at this point?

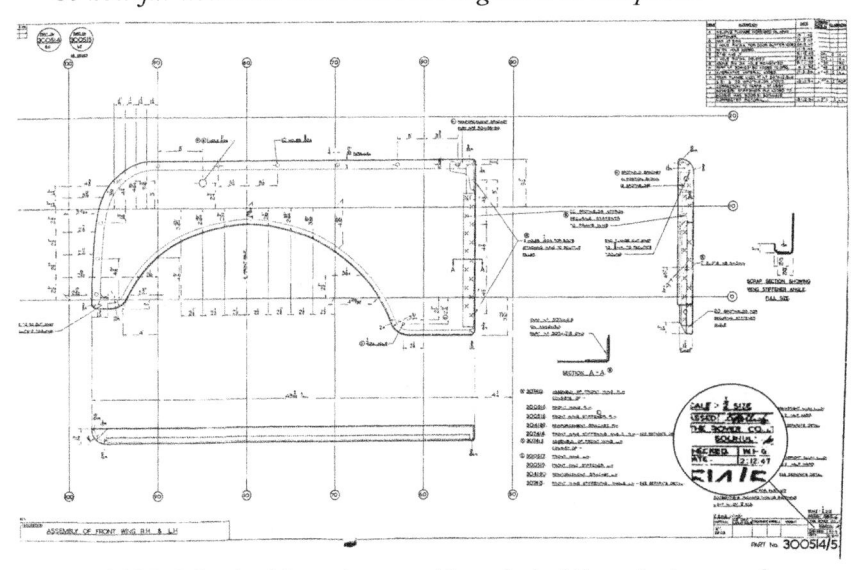

Part 300542 the bulkhead support bracket of the windscreen from 10/12/1947 with update on the 28/04/1948

The drawing of part 300542 or the to bulkhead support bracket for the windscreen frame was drawn on 10/12/47 but a note added on 28/04/48 that mentions 'This piece may not be required when the one piece dash is introduced' referring to the up and coming 'Pressed Bulkhead'. Now, this is two days before the Amsterdam Motor Show, when the Land Rover was

Michael Bishop

officially released!! Arthur had told us that by the time of the show they were extremely confident that they had a huge hit with the Land Rover already on there hands. Seeing that at this point the engineers are at the initial stage of planning the pressed bulkhead for real mass production then no doubt they did have some big orders already in. The first pressed bulkhead vehicle R861501 was dispatched 'In' on 17/12/48, nearly 8 months later!!

One of the other items we know was on L05 when it was built were the through dash controls which a few theories have been discussed over the years. At this point was the intention to have the trough dash or ring pull?

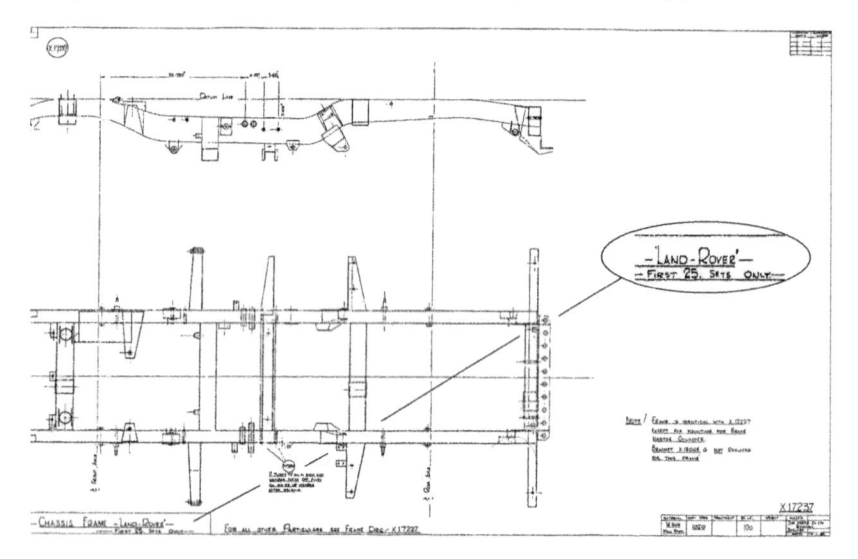

Part X12137, early pre production chassis from 12/01/1948

Well on the same day as the pressed bulkhead note was made on 300542, drawing 218030 was done of the 'General Arrangement of Chassis'. In the drawing you can see all the normal production parts, exhaust, oil filler position, radiator and ring pull freewheel control. Certainly the engineers were well ahead of the game and the Pre Production vehicles were simply in many cases being assembled with what they had already had or produced but like the centre steer before hand. The quirky bits days, like the Centre Steers days were numbered. Any idea of it being a stop gap had obviously long gone. Looking back from this point back to September and October 1947. Did they have the time or even reason to go to the trouble to make up more centre steer vehicles? Highly doubt it. We know already that they had a number of complete chassis to choose from as R16's Chassis is build number '38' and L29's chassis build

They Found Our Engineer

number is maybe, closer to the bottom of the pile, being '16' and they were even assembled at the point the drawing was made.

So many of the participants of the dinner were a touch surprised by these revelations. At the bar after the dinner many of us had a long discussion over what this all meant to our previous understanding of the Land Rover Project. The evening was a success.

Certainly Land Rover had been kind in giving me a few extra significant drawings and I would add a good one to the next article I wrote.

I was also given drawing X17237 from 12/01/48 which is of the Pre Production Chassis frame for vehicles with the so called 'Lockheed' brakes. Note the drawing says 'first 25 sets' and also that the frame is the same as X17227 and that master cylinder bracket X18065 G was not required. Also down the side that tubes X17850 are added which we know are for the other master cylinder.

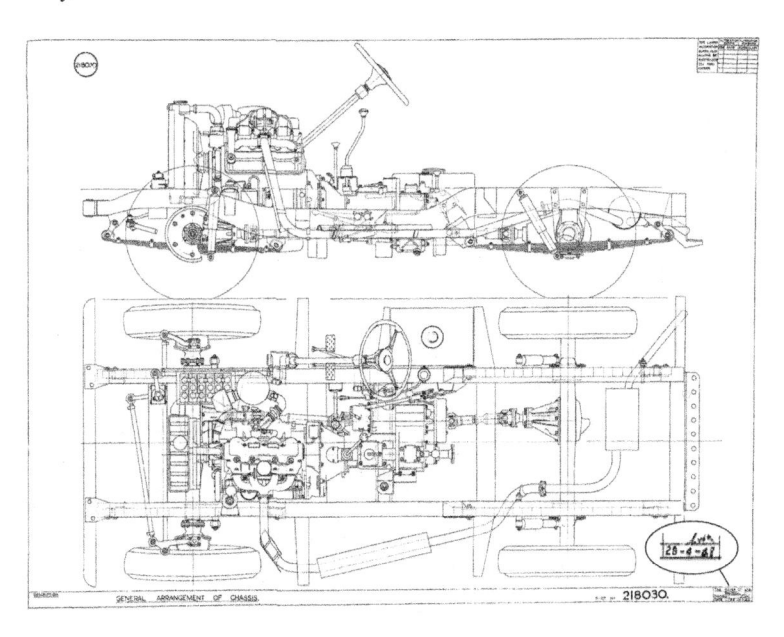

Part 218030 General chassis arrangement for production from 28/04/1948

With the 25 sets for this chassis gives us a clue as to where they were heading but the lower number of the 'Girling brakes' chassis certainly suggests as Arthur said, Girling were the only brakes considered by Rover. The Lockheed type we know were used not for very long. But back to the build numbers of R16 and L29. L29 certainly has two galvanised in place Girling Master Cylinder Brackets for Left and Right hand drive options and R16 was clearly noted as many of the earlier pre pros with a later welded in Girling bracket and only on the Right being a right hand drive. But what about the build numbers of the two chassis as mentioned before?

Your guess is as good as mine. We need drawing X17227 to get a few more clues on this.

So we can now put a few more Early Land Rover Myths to bed. Certainly once Arthur and the team really got into it, clearly the real Land Rover was no stop gap. But we just can't go and completely bin these tales. Certainly they really must relate to only the very early centre steer stage which we know was a very simple stage at the start of the story. But when did Arthur first see the centre steer? Well he tells us as a complete vehicle. He was at that stage in charge of the research lab and along with Robert Boyle, Arthur was the only other broad range Engineer. All the rest of the team were specialists in their own areas. Being a new project and not car based Arthur got the job. So the Centre Steer was a Maurice Wilks thing that was very early 'playing with the idea'. With his own Jeep? Well we can't be sure of that yet. Arthur says they were shown the vehicle and it took no time to get rid of that idea and they didn't think about it too much after that. Like many development vehicles it was simply a means to an end and once that 5 minutes was up and they started thinking about the real Land Rover to be designed, so the start of the beginning of end for the Centre Steer.

The Full Grille Team.

Arthur had his say too with a toast to the Land Rover. We collected questions from enthusiasts for Arthur to answer. All had a drink, a chat and a few laughs. When it came to the technical side, we came to appreciate that Arthur Goddard, the engineer, is the man who always looks forward to the next design and solving the next problem and didn't stand still too long. He shocked the evening's 80" loving crowd when asked if he had his time again what would he change to which he answered "Get rid of the 80" and start with the 86" as it was overall a better design." This comment was characteristic of Arthur, the engineer. Call it 'cold blooded' but Arthur believes that if you let emotion get into your engineering designs, you will never move forward to the bigger and better solutions. Arthur also knows full well that to progress to the 86" and 107" they had to learn all they could from the 80." Given that, the 80" had been a great design and the right design for its time.

The follow up

And the research continues. Spen was 100% right about not being able "to touch the sides" with respect to the history of a company like Rover. Being able to dig deeper is all part of the fun. It was great for Land Rover enthusiasts to have the opportunity to have suspected beliefs confirmed and myths dispelled by the last surviving engineer of the original Land Rover project. Arthur was his usual self. He has an incisive memory packed full of engineering detail. In one instance, he was asked about the early Land Rover drum brakes, the unusual self-adjusting, hydrastatic type. Arthur was right on the button again. He explained that Scott Ivason patented the basic concept and that static meant that the wheel cylinder hardly moves. Ivason invented the return spring in the leading shoe, but the hydrastatic brakes can wear very quickly. When the drum develops an internal wear ridge it is extremely difficult to remove it, making it difficult to dismantle on this design. These are problems that those of us of who use them know well. Dave and I eventually found Scott Ivason's patent, dated April 20th 1927. This was way before Arthur's time, but Ivason's concept was just as Arthur had described. After all, Arthur had been the technical director of Girling Brakes for well over decade. And we know he knows his stuff inside out. Two club members from Belgium, Johan and Tom attended the dinner, and Arthur spoke further about the vehicles in Belgium and the local gendamerie who used them. Arthur had a great story about getting lost when testing a Land Rover in a Belgium forest. They mistakenly crossed the border and ended up in Germany. They got into a touch of strife having a military test vehicle on the wrong side of the border post without the necessary paperwork!

Dave though got 'the prize' story from Arthur. He found out the reason behind the layout for the controls of the first prototype four wheel drive. Unusually these came through the dashboard instead of through the driver's floor. Arthur explained that they had a bloke who had started working with them on ergonomics. The bloke wanted to have the floor clear of all obstructions, and took this to the extreme. He didn't last long and this design was soon changed. On a number of previous occasions, Alex and I had tried to have Arthur to explain this to us, but perhaps we weren't clear enough in what we asked. The magazine articles from the day at Solihull were fantastic too. *Classic and Sports Car* had the renowned car photographer, James Mann take pictures for the day. These stunning pictures were taken from in and around the factory and the old test runs.

I kept trawling through the drawings Roger had sent, looking for early dates for the 80", 86" and Series or Mark 2. I was planning to visit Arthur in Australia later in the year and wanted to have some questions ready. In the footage that Graeme Aldous filmed, Arthur had given a particularly short but interesting answer to a question from James Taylor in regards to Rover's stylist, David Bache. Bache is credited with the Series 2 Land Rover styling, which is still currently used on the Defender. Another clue luckily appeared at the Series One club committee meeting in September. It was a clue relating to the first prototype 86." In anticipation of Arthur's visit, I had been looking for "P86/1." The earliest known drawings for it are from late 1950. It is easy to see the care taken in the design of 86" and appreciate the time it took. This was in stark comparison to the urgency of the 80". P86/1 re appeared again just after Arthur left as a result of an enquiry to the 86" technical officer of the Series 1 club. Again, pure Land Rover gold. The vehicle had unusually high body sides and doors compared to production models. It had me itching to ask Arthur about it. Had the high sides influenced the Series 2 design in anyway? The capping line on the Series 2 is much higher than a standard short wheelbase Series 1. Arthur had already told us the process that they used to make the P86/1. The production method was fairly simple and was still used, years after his time. Using simple hand sketches, drawings and calculations, the engineers would lay out the components and construct the vehicle in the engineering department. This was followed by a discussion with the drawing office about the plans and official drawings needed for the new parts. Once the drawings were done, they all met again. This was to make sure that the drawings fully met the engineers' specifications and nothing had been mistakenly changed in the drawing. The drawings would then be signed off.

High sided prototype 86" P86/1

Michelle and I returned to Australia to see family and friends. We had a great time. I visited Brisbane to see Arthur and Alex's family. I also saw and a good mate, Taz, who has a beautifully restored early Queensland CKD Land Rover that we had used for a few photos with Arthur early on. I visited the Goddard factory and saw the engineering toys there. Some of the trailer components they make are quite exceptional. Arthur's younger son Chris had just returned from England. We had a great laugh about the adventure we all had with Arthur's story. Arriving in Brisbane was just a continuation of the fun.

Arthur and I discussed other bits and pieces we had found about his later days at Rover. With respect to the P86/1 photos, the idea of having high sides came about quite early on. Arthur recalled that Johnny Cullen had been keen on high sides after the engineers all kept falling out the back of the vehicles with the standard sides. But the design didn't quite work out. Cullen knew that it was much easier to ride in the back of a 104" pick up with high sides. I wondered had this design influenced the roll down side of the Series 2? Arthur explained this one too, and there was no doubt. When designer David Bache started, he and Maurice did a comprehensive redesign of everything at Rover and the Land Rover was no different. High sides were felt to be needed on all the vehicles and doors. The roll down the side of the bodywork was a brilliant way to make that feature work. Once again, another fascinating insight into how quickly a decision could be made and shared. The 107" Station Wagons always looked 'interesting' with the combination of high and low front doors and high rear doors. The high rear doors were necessary because the rear passengers sit up a little higher than the front passengers. The roll in the side made the long wheel base Station Wagon design work very well. It is possible to see last evidence of the higher doors in the long wheelbase station wagons of the 1960s, 1970s and early 1980s. The rear door handle is fitted in a higher position than the front ones. Later door handles in the 1980's fixed that anomaly. Arthur shared that widening the Land Rover from the roll in the body work for the Series 2 caused issues for off road driving and for the military, but this was a decision he could not change.

I also had a few other items for him to think about. Having studied over 2500 factory drawings, two appeared that proved what Arthur had told us about the Centre Steer and the speed in which the design came about. The first picture is of Part 219646 horn and head lamp harness for the Land Rover dated 8 October 1947. This was an almost impossibly early date for the 80" Land Rover that needed more than just a second glance. Lucas supplied the electrical wiring harnesses and system. This showed how vital it was from the onset to make sure that Land Rover's suppliers fully understood what was needed - common sense approach.

They Found Our Engineer

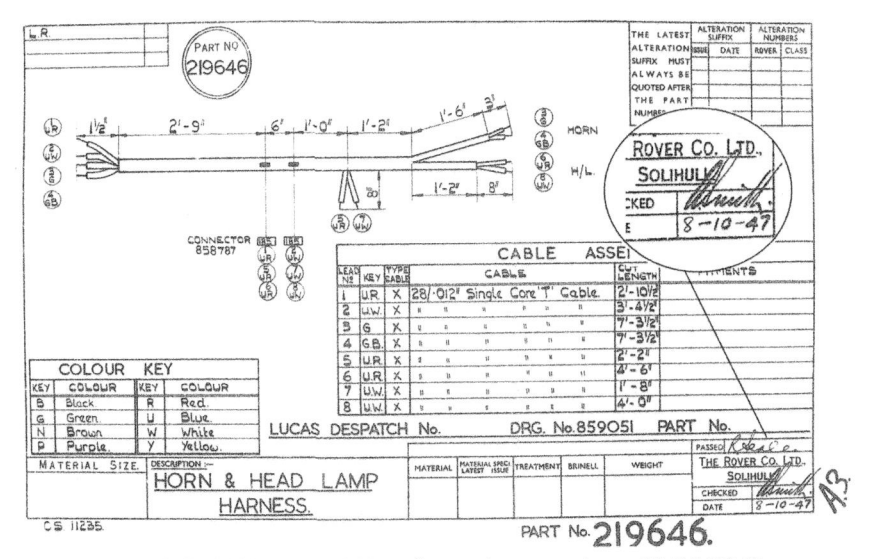

Part 219646 Horn and Headlamp harness from 08/10/1947

    That date confirms that Arthur was right in his conclusion that the centre steering idea was not considered fully. The Rover photograph ledger in 1947 includes two photographs of particular relevance between 23 and 30 September 1947 - one of the Centre Steer chassis and a second photo of a near complete but unpainted vehicle. This was around a week or two before Part 219646 horn and head lamp harness, the earliest known Land Rover part was drawn. The evidence that Land Rover parts were drawn up this early shows that the engineering team started the design straight away.

    The Centre Steer was photographed again as 'complete' on the 15 October 1947. This was when the "real" Land Rover was being designed and laid out. The Rover board met the next day on 16th October and heard a bit more about the *'Landrover'* that a *'pre-production batch of fifty was already in progress.'* The second set of very early drawing to appear includes the drawings for Parts 217571, 217572 and 217573 - front, rear and power take off propeller shafts. Hardy Spicer supplied these parts with the drawings are dated 3 November1947. There is no doubt that most of 80" Land Rover's dimensions were set by this point.

Michael Bishop

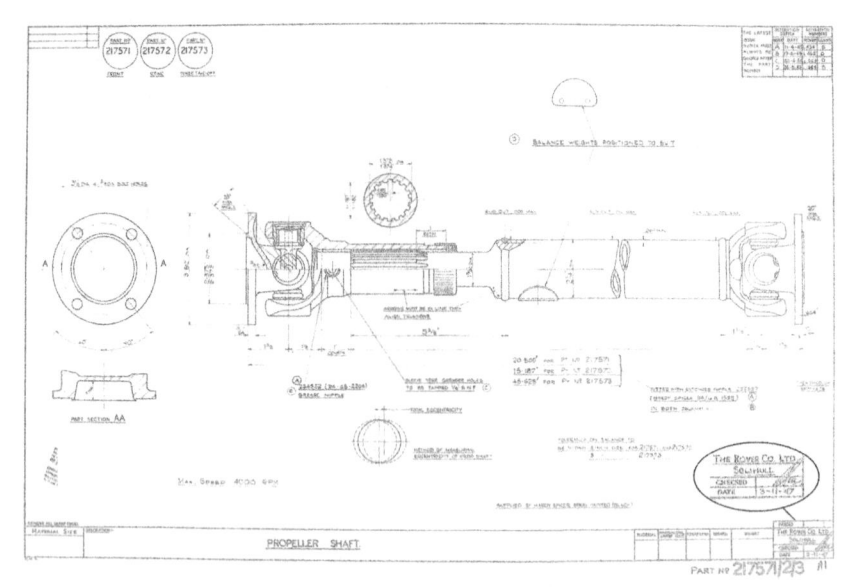

Parts 217571 to 217573 from 03/11/1947

When presented with the drawings and the implications of them, Arthur just smiled and said "I told you so." We proved that he was right about the Centre Steer, and that the Land Rover project team hadn't taken much of it into consideration in the design of the Series 1 Land Rover. Arthur shared that getting your suppliers on board was one of the first and most important tasks. For Lucas, designing and making up the initial wiring looms was a complicated process. Lucas was usually the first to see a new design. Having received the initial dimensions and a design brief on a new vehicle, they laid the wiring loom on a huge board. Hardy Spicer wouldn't have been too far behind them. This showed how fast and effective the simple engineering decision making process that the Wilks brother had in place worked.

Arthur and one of development vehicles from 1948 that was dispatched directly to him, with current owner Colin Howe who has owned this Land Rover since the late 1950's

Back in England a few weeks later, I called Roger to share these exciting developments. Roger and James Taylor had formed the opinion from what Arthur had said about the Centre Steer, that from the very beginning, the Land Rover development had intersected and run parallel with the Centre steer program for a short time. We now know that this is in no doubt the case. Roger had seen the pictures of the development of Land Rover P86/1 and it did all make sense. Even the width issues. Roger said that the edge above the roll side of the post Series 2 Land Rovers is the same width on a Defender as it was on a Series 1. To this Roger added that the extra width was an issue with the Ministry of Defence and in the 1960s Land Rover nearly put the 80" back in production for the military. Upon inspecting the now old 80" chassis jigs at Solihull, it was found that the jigs had been recently cut up and disposed of. So the Land Rover Lightweight was made instead. It was known that this vehicle wasn't really light in weight as a complete vehicle, but it was just as narrow as a Series 1. And that is what the Ministry of Defence wanted in their vehicles at the time.

Thanks to Arthur we now have a much broader and deeper understanding of Land Rover's early days, how the vehicle we all know so well was designed and how the design evolved so quickly. As well, we know that the original team applied the original Land Rover design from

1948 to the Series 2, and the design is still very much part of the Land Rover Defender. The 'stop gap' story has its place at the very start of the Land Rover, in the Centre Steer vehicle itself. In many ways the Centre Steer can also be considered a stop gap between Maurice Wilks' idea and the true Land Rover. Thanks to the dynamic team at Rover back then, we know now how the Centre Steer fits in and makes up a small but still important part of the Land Rover Legend today.

An Afternoon Chat with Spen and Arthur

Spen King played a pivotal role in validating Arthur's story. We met in the very early stages of Arthur coming to light and spent a pleasant afternoon discussing their memories of working for Rover in the 1940s and 1950s.

Spen King at the driver's seat of Rover's Jet1 the first Gas Turbine Car. Arthur can be seen walking up to the car. Spencer and Maurice Wilks watch on

Spen told about the fun the engineers had after work playing with the various "toys" that their colleagues had made or were working on. He also confirmed a few of the stories. Having not seen his former colleague for many years, when Arthur arrived back in England, he said he would like to say hello to catch up over a cup of tea. This is something that we all do. We believe it was in the late 1960s that they had last seen each other. This is when Arthur, as Girling technical director, met Rover to discuss using Girling brakes on the up and coming Range Rover.

While Arthur, Alex and I were running about here and there, I took a moment to give Spen a call and ask if it was ok for us to call by. Spen was pleased to hear Arthur was about and had heard he was coming to England. Spen invited us to drop by for tea that afternoon. On the phone, Spen mentioned he was recovering from an eye operation. He didn't want any fuss with cameras as he wasn't at his best. This was a welcome opportunity for us to have a break from filming. When we arrived, Spen looked great. He had removed his eye patch and was ready for an entertaining hour or so.

I was looking forward to hearing the two of them chat about the times of old and all that. We had gone as a pure social visit. It was not meant to be an interview. As we also know now, Arthur's historic bombshells drop left, right and centre. So with Spen's and Arthur's agreement, we kept sound recording just in case.

We could not forsee how fate was going to play out. About a month after our visit, Spen had a cycling accident which sadly resulted in his death.

This chat between Arthur and Spen is a classic. You can feel that fun and vibrant place that the post war Rover Company was. It shines brightly through with Arthur and Spen. Alex and I felt that this unique insight into two engineering greats was best shared. Special thanks to Spen's family for allowing us to share his words here.

Spen King:	So, who have you been seeing Arthur?
Arthur Goddard	I've been everywhere and (seen) everything and everybody I think the last 3 or 4 days
Spen:	Have you?
Arthur	I've seen more of Land Rover than I saw of it in 10 years.

They Found Our Engineer

Spen:	Really? I still go on a sort of annual lunch that goes on, and there's about 60 or 70 people there. It's absolutely magic.
Arthur	Mmm.
Spen:	You know, after a bit they start disappearing until they drop off. (laughs)
Arthur	I found my old office, which was a start.
Spen:	What?
Arthur	I found my old office where I used to live.
Spen:	Did you?
Arthur	Yeah.
Spen:	Good lord. When did you clear off out of the Rover company? What year was it?
Arthur	It would have been round towards about 1960.
Spen:	The 50s.
Arthur	No, I think 45, it would be approaching 1960.
Spen:	I would guess, yeah.
Arthur	I'm glad I got out to miss some of Lord Stokes' antics.
Spen:	Thank God you missed that. That would have been a good thing to miss.
Arthur	I think it was a good thing to miss, wasn't it?
Spen:	Oh, it really was.
Arthur	So I thought I had a bit of luck there. I went to the factory and I went upstairs over the main office. And I don't think I've ever been upstairs over the main office.
Spen:	Haven't you?
Arthur	No. (laughs) There was nobody up there that I really had much to do with I think. Spence Wilks and a gentleman called Savage and I wasn't sure whether he was or he wasn't.
Spen:	So, you've done rather well, I sort of had understood over the years. You've got your own company?
Arthur	Yes, well my son has more or less taken it off me now.
Spen:	Right.
Arthur	But yes, it's going strength to strength.
Spen:	What does it do? I know it involves engineering intelligence of some sort?
Arthur	We're in caravans and trailers, up to about 5 tonnes.
Spen:	Yes.

Michael Bishop

Arthur looking at a chassis with Alex looking on.

Arthur	And we make suspensions and couplings and jacking systems.
Spen:	I see, ok. How many people do you employ?
Arthur	Oh, at the moment about 28.
Spen:	And you know what each one individually is doing, which is really good.
Arthur	(laughs) You have to be careful when you go much bigger. You go much bigger then you don't know everybody and trouble starts. (laughs)
Spen:	Yes, exactly. It gets out of control because somebody starts worming away.
Arthur	So, we've got a few of the family there. Chris is running it. And I'm still doing the engineering but mainly advanced engineering.
Spen:	Like what?
Arthur	And I've got three assistants who look after day to day and keep the machines running and investigate minor things that come along. But I've organised it rather well; I only do exactly what I like doing. (laughs)
Spen:	Yeah, I'm not winking at you. I'm protecting this eye.
Arthur	You're doing well.

Arthur	And Chris's wife helps with the wages. One of the grandsons is pretty heavy with these computer-controlled machines which seem to take a fair bit of looking after from what I can work out. (laughs) When they're good they're very, very good but when they're bad oh dear. (laughs)
Spen:	This is the world we're living in now, isn't it?
Arthur	For some reason when we're coming to your house I was thinking of a wooden house that's built on top of some walls and making it a two storey, a wooden bungalow.
Spen:	Peter Wilks had a house.
Arthur	Peter. That's what it could be. Yes.
Spen:	He called it after the people who made those houses, those sort of prefabricated.
Arthur	That's right, but I heard he stood it on top of foundations.
Spen:	No, I don't think he did. He was, you know you look at it from lower down. It was up the hill basically.
Arthur	It stood up like that.
Spen:	Anyway, that was a long time ago sadly.
Spen:	It was sad too. Robert Boyle had a lot to do with it I guess. (laughs) I remember, very well and Gallaford with his stomach who ran the shop. (laughs) Paddy, I remember a few people from those days.
Arthur	I've had a lot of fun out of the motor industry. I think it's a great place to work.
Spen:	Well, it can be. What it's like these days I don't know. I got out of it a long time ago.
Arthur	You had a pretty good time. You had an interesting time with that turbine. What's his name, Frank Bell?
Spen:	Frank Bell. That's right.
Arthur	And was Noel Penny involved in that at one stage?
Spen:	He was involved for a long time, and he ended up running his own company.
Arthur	And he's still successful is he?
Spen:	No, it's not successful. He went bust.
Arthur	It must be easy to do it. Fortunately I haven't found out how to do it yet. (laughs)

Spen:	What, going bust? (laughs) I suspect there's bad ways and good ways of doing it. (laughs)
Arthur	We stick very closely to things that we know what we're doing.
Spen:	It's a very good idea.
Arthur	Every time I've invested money and speculation I've come unstuck.
Spen:	Thinking something's a good idea.
Arthur	Oh yes.
Spen:	Well one thing we get terribly wrong, you have a good idea or somebody else does. And it really is a good idea, but you get the timing wrong by years. And it's no good.
Arthur	It's like you're either 100 years late or early and it's equally difficult to deal with.
Spen:	I thought a long, long time ago, I don't know, 30 years ago. I was hoping that these lithium iron batteries were going to be very important. And I bought some stock and that. And they were worth nothing at all. But now of course, it's a really big thing.
Arthur	Well, I would say my judgement on what will be a success and a failure is not all that good.
Spen:	You can't tell.
Arthur	I've made some hideous mistakes. (laughs) Some people are good at it.
Spen:	Well, lucky.
Arthur	Maurice was good at it.
Spen:	Who?
Arthur	Maurice Wilks.
Spen:	Was he? He was wrong with gas turbines.
Arthur	Well, he appeared to pick things that sold. Didn't he?
Spen:	Yes.
Arthur	Everything that I worked on that he came up with (laughs) was a winner. So if you can do that, you don't have to be clever or anything else, do you?
Spen:	No. I think the family management of the Rover Company was not too bad.

Arthur	It was very good. It was excellent. You see, they had enough sense to surround themselves with some pretty good people you know, like Farmer and AB Smith and these chaps you know.
Spen:	Mmm.
Arthur	George Seal and Jack Swaine. But they don't grow on trees. And that was why the Land Rover was such an easy job for me because I had all these guys who knew what they were doing.
Spen:	Line up to do the dirty work.
Arthur	(laughs) All sitting there ready to go. It couldn't have been done. We had a big lump of empty factory and all these fellas, specialists and various things. And about oh 50% or 60% of the engineering we just took them from the cars anyway. Engines and gear boxes and various things. So it was not an earth shattering event like some people think it was.
Spen:	But basically Rover was there with the Jeep anyway.
Arthur	Yes, that told me that most of the bits that were available from the car factory, from old Tony Worcester.
Spen:	And you only had to fill it with aluminium rivets. (laughs)
Arthur	And all the bends were straight lines. (laughs)
Spen:	It's got better looking year after year as it's went on. (laughs)
Arthur	That all worked out rather well in the end. But people I've talked to here and that they all give the impression that they thought it (Rover's Factory) was an open field. You suddenly produced all this stuff out of nowhere.
Spen:	You've got to have things to pick up and use if you're working in there.
Arthur	A lot of things to pick up and a lot of jolly good fellas knew what they were doing, you see. You see fellas like Bashford, you see. Great job.
Spen:	Who?
Arthur	Gordon.

Spen:	Gordon Bashford. Oh, indeed yes. Terrific bloke. The same thing really happened with Range Rover you see which was my particular thing. You had to pick up things which were already there and put them in- a way that probably would sell and that was it.
Arthur	That was great, really it was good fun. And because you could get decisions, like all the bosses were on the premises.
Spen:	You could get what?
Arthur	Decisions.
Spen:	Oh yes.
Arthur	Because getting decisions if you're an engineer is the most difficult part of the job.
Spen:	Yes, product policies.
Arthur	I'm sure if you were chasing Mr Stokes it would be very different from going in and asking Robert Boyle.
Spen:	Very different, yeah.
Arthur	It would take you three weeks to find him (Stokes) to start with I'd say.
Arthur	But that was the great thing you see. Whatever it was, if you got stuck, as soon as you'd figured out what to do to get out of it, you could get the decision right away to either do it or not do it or clear off or something. But you'd get the decision
Spen:	The other thing which went along with that was it was a good company to work for and people enjoyed their work.
Arthur	They did. Certainly, they did. Yes, it's great. And then it all got blown apart in 2 or 3 easy years.
Spen:	What, by BL you mean?
Arthur	Oh, it was one after the other. Wasn't it with that lot? I was very friendly with Bob Knight who was the chief executive at Jag.
Spen:	Oh yes. Were you, yes?
Arthur	He used to cry in my beer.

They Found Our Engineer

Arthur's Factory Tour at Land Rover in 2010.

Spen:	Bob could cry at great lengths too. You were really wet. (laughs) I remember Bob saying after one of these ghastly all company meetings they tried to do management by exhortation and it doesn't work. That was what Bob said. And he was right.
Arthur	When you think people have all disappeared you know over that set up, you know. Sid Eliver at MG, he ran his complete with MG. There was Riley; I forgotten who owned Riley.
Spen:	It wasn't a person.
Arthur	Charlie Griffin who ran Wolseley.
Spen:	They had already been gobbled into the Morris empire you see.
Arthur	And they're all gone. It's absolutely amazing. (laughs) I can't talk because Lucas has disappeared as well. (laughs)
Spen:	Well, you've outlived them. You had the lab (at Rover), the first empire wasn't it?
Arthur	Yes, I was playing about with that. Did a bit on balancing on the turbine and a bit on high energy spark. Well I was the fella who has the electronics guys. (laughs)

Spen:	I know you put strange edges on rockers or something like that and produced the power to do with the ignition.
Arthur	When you've got the electronics guy (laughs) you're in the crown seat. Well him, a good tin basher like our big panel beater fella. That would also put you in some good positions. If people wanted to see what a different wing looked like, you know, amazing, he'd put in rollers and so on.
Spen:	Poppe's jig shop it was called.
Arthur	Yes, that's right. He did a good job on the Land Rover old Poppe.
Spen:	He did a job of that Poppe.
Spen:	Well he invented the Land Rover chassis frame.
Arthur	He did, yes.
Arthur	Not only sure if he invented it, but he invented how to put it together.
Spen:	I mean they built them. Gordon drew them up, and tested them for stiffness. And learnt the fundamentals of what cross members did the job and all that sort of thing, and it was very much Poppe
Arthur	Well it would be the most torsionally stiff chassis that ever went onto a vehicle I should think. It was a beauty. It never gave any trouble, not as far as I can remember anyway and would only rust away in the end.
Spen:	I think the intention really was to zinc coat it all over.
Arthur	Yeah, well we did for quite a few.
Spen:	But then it was sorted I think.
Arthur	And then somebody had the bright idea that this paint was, if you dipped it in the paint was just as good, but it wasn't.
Spen:	No.
Arthur	But it was so much easier and so much nicer and so on, you see. Because the stuff you were dipping in wasn't red hot (laughs) which helps. I could well see why people were enthusiastic about it, but it was nothing like it. Well even today there's nothing touches hot dip galvanising if you don't want it to rust

Arthur	We haven't improved on it in 100 years.
Spen:	Yes, all to do with electrolysis and that sort of stuff.
Arthur	Are you still working?
Spen:	No, only working at existing that's all really. And you're working, you are?
Arthur	I work about I suppose about I suppose 35 hours a week.
Spen:	Is your brother still alive?
Arthur	Oh yes.
Spen:	The one I remember.
Arthur	Yes. He used to be a bit with you on you on the turbines didn't he?
Spen:	He was around though, yes. What's his name?
Arthur	Les.
Spen:	Les. That's right.
Arthur	He's coming down next Friday he tells me. He's even older than me would you believe? I didn't think there was anybody older than me. He's older. He's 5 years older.
Spen:	How old are you then?
Arthur	I'm 90 in January.
Spen:	Are you really? I thought you were older than me. But I didn't know by how much.
Arthur	You're only a youngster. Were one of our promising young fellas. (laughs)
Spen:	That's right. (laughs)
Arthur	One of our young men of potential we called them. (laughs)
Spen:	Where do you live in Oz?
Arthur	I live in Brisbane.
Arthur	It's nice and slow there, not too exciting and not too much.
Spen:	It's pretty hot down there a lot of the time, is a good excuse to take it slowly.
Arthur	It's an interesting one, because it doesn't get as hot in Sydney and Melbourne.
Spen:	Is it humid?

Michael Bishop

Arthur	It's not bad, except in a couple of months where you (sweat), but it appears to be a much steadier. (than Sydney or Melbourne) Summer and winter are pretty much the same, rather than Melbourne that gets hotter than us and colder than us.
Spen:	But in Melbourne each day's different from the next one really or every half day's different from the previous one.
Alex Massey	I wouldn't know about that.
Spen:	You live out there?
Michael Bishop:	Yeah, oh yeah.
Arthur	Life's quite a bit of fun at the moment, especially that so called recession. I mean we're all waiting for it, plan this and plan that (laughs) and plan the other, if this happens and if this happens.
Spen:	My father was born in Melbourne believe it or not.
Arthur	Was he?
Spen:	He was, yes. At least he had two passports.
Arthur	I've got two. But the fella in Australia didn't like the English one. So he gave me it back and took the Aussie one to let me out. He held it (the English passport) up to his machine, and it sort of went fizz you see.
Spen:	It probably ran out about 40 years ago. (Everyone laughs.)
Arthur	No, I've been good. I've been staying with my sister-in-law who's got a nice house, very convenient for chasing Land Rovers.
Spen:	Where's that?
Arthur	In Kenilworth, yeah, very handy. I've got quite a bit to do now til Friday. I'll (will) be looking forward to going round the engineering department of Land Rover which I've been invited to do I think.
Spen:	That will be interesting.
Arthur	Oh, it will. I'm surprised they let me but eh, not too surprised.
Spen:	I don't think there are many secrets there that you're thinking about.

Arthur	Mmmm, well we've been driving a little Land Rover which is, what is it called?
Michael:	A Freelander.
Arthur	Freelander.
Spen:	Oh yes.
Michael:	Roger lent us one.
Spen:	The Freelander too is a big thing. And it's as big as the Range Rover as far as I can see. It's a giant monster. It's a nice refined vehicle.
Arthur	One I was going to ask you as I've been trying to find out. When you look at that and say that's a Land Rover, how do you define what the difference is between a Land Rover and a Range Rover? This thing's got everything but bells and whistles. (laughs) And it's just a four wheel drive car.
Spen:	Well, I suppose Range Rover is now a Land Rover with a high price on (sic).
Arthur	(laughs)
Spen:	I don't know. One thing that I think is terribly important in a vehicle, if you're going to use it a lot is road noise. And whether the Range Rover is appreciably quieter I don't know, because it's got an integral frame and everything this thing.
Arthur	We had a good range of noisy tyres in my day. If you wanted to get rid of road noise, you got rid of those noisy tyres, number one.
Spen:	Well that's number one. That's different. That's tread noise. That's tyre noise and maybe.
Arthur	You mean actual road surface noise?
Spen:	Road surface noise is the thing. If you live on motorways, you'll spend your whole life being deafened by the road noise, you know, in almost all modern vehicles.
Arthur	Really?
Spen:	Yeah.
Arthur	We don't appear to have that problem, do we (in Australia)?
Spen:	I think this vehicle is really quite good.

Michael Bishop

Arthur's Factory Tour at Land Rover in 2010.

Michael:	Yeah, it's very quiet inside. It's a diesel, so you can hear a little bit of engine noise.
Spen:	But it doesn't worry you, does it?
Michael:	No, it's not oppressive.
Spen:	Road noise, if you are going on a long motorway for instance, you can't do anything about it. You've got the damn thing whether you like it or not. You can't talk. You're not listening to the radio. And it's tiring. But this thing, I think is good.
Arthur	And you can't get out of it by going faster. (Everyone laughs.)
Spen:	No, you can't. You can stop.
Arthur :	Stop. (laughs) Yes, that's good (the Freelander).
Spen:	But I think you pointed out something. But you see people want fancy vehicles. If they've got cash, their vehicle is their toy and they want to have the most expensive, so they go and buy a Range Rover. It really is true.
Arthur :	Well they certainly sell don't they? I don't know what the export sales look like or what the model split is on sales.

They Found Our Engineer

Spen:	Well Range Rover does terribly well in America because they've got so much money and people want to spend money on a toy. And they want the most expensive toy
Arthur:	That's not a bad business to be in is it? (laughs)
Spen:	Very good, but have it backed up by something which you can make much cheaper is the Freelander really. Where they're going now I don't know, I think they may be going to use the Jaguar aluminium structure thing, bonded riveted.
Arthur:	That big press is a frightening thing isn't it?
Spen:	Which?
Arthur:	The big press in the factory of Land Rover in Solihull. This massive press which they're using for all sorts of things like.
Spen:	I don't know. I haven't seen it. I'm not let into the secrets of the factory like you are or anything.
Arthur:	You wouldn't want to see it. £90 million pounds.
Spen:	What?
Arthur:	You can't credit it can you? They had to dig a hole 100 ft deep or something and put in 27,000 tonnes of concrete.
Spen:	Is it working now?
Arthur:	Oh yes.
Spen:	Oh good.
Arthur:	And this was all to do with they weren't allowed to have any vibration. I said then why did you put it in the middle of Solihull? If you didn't want any vibration, where there's a lot of England where you can put it somewhere where nobody cares how much you do.
Spen:	Anyway they've done it, they're in the middle of Solihull.
Arthur:	They've done it. Of course the vibrations cost as much as the original estimate you see. Once it went wrong, and I must say whatever they've done there's very little vibration.
Michael:	There's none virtually.
Spen:	What parts do they make? Do they make a whole lot of pressings simultaneously on one stroke?

Arthur:	No, it's about a three stage transfer press. And they're making the complete side of the Range Rover. But of course, it's incredible really, because the first thing it comes out it goes plonk. And it blanks out about half the material and sends it downstairs to the scrap, you see. So you're thinking my goodness. And when you're finished, you've got a little bit that goes right round everything and all the rest is in the pit where it's got sixteen trucks in the road taking the scrap out
Spen:	That's right. All you want to do is the factory next door will take the scrap and turn it into sheet metal and start all over again
Arthur :	The man said to me, he said, Of course, anybody trying to compete with this….
Spen:	It all depends on the whim of the customer actually. Somebody must have been bloody brave to put that much money into a hole.
Arthur :	Fortunately it was put in by BMW. And I should think a few weeks after they'd spend their £90 mil they sold it to somebody else for about a tenner.
Michael:	They put it in the early 2000s. And it's just enormous.
Arthur :	I think what happened was they got the bill for it, don't you?
Spen:	I've got a BMW pension. I don't like them chucking mine in. (laughs)
Arthur :	So that really is huge. You wouldn't believe it would you?
Michael:	I had no idea they had anything quite like that on the site.
Arthur :	Completely dumbfounded, yeah.
Michael:	When we walked in and saw it.
Spen:	How big is it? As big as this room?
Michael:	It's as big as this house. It's enormous.
Spen:	As big as the house, well it would be for £90 mil.
Arthur :	A set of tools cost half a million pounds. And they can just about fit in this office, in this room. That space, solid whatever it is, it's got a few little lumps and bumps on it.
Spen:	And then they pick them up.

Arthur :	Well, they get a crane. A crane costs about £10 mil to fix up this lot . And brings it down and lowers it down and locates it onto the things. And then it goes across and goes underneath a big section in the centre and underneath the press. And then, by some magic, they've succeeded in taking these great big things off that are already on and putting these on in their place. But it isn't a sort of 10 minute change over by the look of it.
Spen:	It isn't.
Arthur :	No, I should think it's a 10 hour change over.
Spen:	Really. I mean with all that, it ought to be a damn quick change. I thought that was the point of it.
Arthur :	There's nothing quick about moving this stuff around.
Michael:	The bloke said to me when they get it all in place, they can actually change the tool in half an hour.
Spen:	That's what I thought they were supposed to do, yeah.
Michael:	Yeah, but I think there's a process of actually getting the tool to the spot where you can do the half an hour. So the process, you know, it is half an hour but it isn't really half an hour. There's a process of getting the tools there.
Arthur :	Yeah, it's a question of whether it works.
Arthur :	It'll be shut down for a lot longer than a half hour.
Michael:	Yeah, exactly.
Arthur :	You've only to look at it. It must have nuts this (huge) diameter. (laughs)
Spen:	It's a question of how many pressings you do on a run. I suppose before you change over to another tool to make something else.
Arthur :	That's what it's all about. And they've got a lot of sets of tools, haven't they? How many have they got there?
Michael:	Well they have all current Range Rovers, Range Rover Sport, and Land Rover Discovery.
Arthur :	Is it only the Alpha ones for some reason?

Michael:	Well, that's that only ones we saw. Apparently they were only running at half production that day. Usually they've got, I don't know…. Obviously, I've only seen it that one day.
Arthur :	If it goes any quicker I wouldn't want to be standing near it, I don't think. (laughs)
Spen:	You'd get the top of your head lopped off.
Michael:	And then the polishing of the tool, if they polish the tool. And they polish the tool every, I can't remember how long it was, but it takes a week to polish it to make sure it's right.
Arthur :	Three tins of Brasso. (laughs)
Michael:	It's a bit more than Brasso, I think. But you know, it's an impressive bit of kit.
Arthur :	Polishing is sort of by hand, I suppose.
Michael:	Yeah. It's all done by hand the polishing.
Arthur :	To say we were impressed was to put it mildly.
Spen:	I think I should arrange to go and see this monster machine.
Arthur :	Oh, you should. It's worth seeing. And it's got a special building, and it's so high, you expect to see clouds. And this massive crane, I think a five hundred tonne crane or something.
Alex:	Fifty tonne.
Spen:	I mean, is this is a gantry thing? This is a thing right across?
Michael:	It's a full remote control one. The guy controlling it just had like one of these, a laptop. You know, a bit stronger and he was controlling it. No lines. No nothing. Controlling it all totally by that.
Spen:	You should hope he doesn't get confused.
Michael:	Yeah. Arthur moved out of the way pretty quickly. (laughs)
Spen:	You could make a wonderful sort of horror film there. (All laugh.)
Arthur :	I have to say it's worth a visit, honestly.

They Found Our Engineer

Arthur's Factory Tour at Land Rover in 2010.

Spen:	Yeah. I will.
Arthur :	And they're quite proud of it.
Spen:	Well they must be, paying that much money. (Arthur laughs)
Arthur :	I think they said there was five of them (worldwide). A Weingarten too. So it wouldn't be cheap. (laughs) They say they've made five of these. I think there is one at Mercedes and one at BMW.
Spen:	They must be able to change pretty smartly to be used in all those places. Because you think of the range of cars that Mercedes make and the cars that BMW make and Land Rover, if there's only four of them, they've got to be changing around them.
Arthur :	I looked at another monster building which seem to be completely full of these pieces (tools). You know, stacked on the ground both ways from here to the end of the street both ways.
Spen:	It's a tool store.

Arthur:	I enquired what about 'just in time' (manufacturing process), you see. Just in time to apply with this press (laughs), you would just run the bloody thing and run the twelve months' supply and then do another twelve months for somebody else. But there's no question of the four days, you know (laughs). It's a good job that Honda had gone before you did that. When you think, you see, it's probably worth about five normal presses this thing. Five normal presses would only have about ten people. So you've gotta go some to get that £90 mil pound back. They'll be getting it back in saving labour, because I'm sure it isn't any quicker because it virtually can't be.
Spen:	I suppose they claim they've got some product that sort of accuracy and things like that come out of it. You know the whole side frame in one go and that sort of thing.
Arthur:	Oh yes. There's no doubt about it. All the holes would be the same size, no argument. They'd load in this huge sheet (of metal), and wham you've got over half of it (waste) going in the cellar. (laughs)
Spen:	Probably more than that. It's a unit body size. Think of the door hole. So it's much more than 50%. This would bring us in from the cellar to the door.
Michael:	That's what they did. And the last pressing of each run, they kept aside for doing, you know, the projection of whether the tool needed polishing in this area or that area or whatever.
Spen:	And measured it up with some fancy machine.
Michael:	Well, they actually had them aside there. They were just doing one from the last run. It was a rear outer panel for a Range Rover Sport. And the bloke was going over with just his marker pen, bit here and there. And I was surprised at how simple that process still was.
Spen:	More sensible.
Michael:	Exactly, yeah.
Arthur:	So, that was the feature of the day I must say.
Spen:	When was that? Yesterday?
Arthur:	That was about a week ago now, wasn't it?
Alex:	Yeah. It was last Friday.

They Found Our Engineer

Arthur :	They're very good. They showed us all around the place and so on, but the site's a bit higgledy piggledy you know.
Spen:	It always was.
Arthur :	Everywhere without rhyme or reason, you know. Your test beds have mostly gone and been replaced.
Spen:	What? The old oval and engine test beds?
Arthur :	Those square things.
Spen:	Wartime meant for Bristol Hercules or something like that.
Arthur :	That's right. Now they knocked down the air raid shelters and knocked down my test track which I had over the top of the air raid shelters. We went to this other place but I haven't seen the people there yet. What do you call it?
Michael:	At Gaydon.
Arthur :	Gaydon.
Michael:	Yeah. The whole (Land Rover office) facility at Gaydon.
Arthur :	Now there, you'd think somebody took a big handful of buildings and threw them down. There must be 30 or 40 buildings. What the hell they all do I don't know. And there's a big car park for everyone of them. There are cars everywhere you look, as far as you can see.
Spen:	What the hell they're doing? Are they really necessary? (in relation to all the cars).
Arthur :	I'm looking forward to find out what it is (laughs), because it seems so crazy. Doesn't it? When you look at it?
Michael:	Well, I've only been in there (once). A friend who was working there got me in on the family and friends day. We didn't even see that other side. We went in the other day because they are restoring an old (Series 1) Land Rover. And they wanted a petrol tank and any of that old stuff they just buy off the clubs and the people that reproduce them. And at the gate they said go down to the near the test track. And we drove through and there were miles of buildings. I knew it was a big facility, but I didn't know it was quite like that.

Arthur:	It's only supposed to be the engineering department and the head office isn't it?
Spen:	Yeah. That's it?
Arthur:	They must have a lot more engineers than I have. (laughs)
Spen:	Say what you like. But it is being successful at the moment anyway. Whether it will go on I don't know, but it is.
Arthur:	If they're making money that's it, isn't it?
Spen:	They increased their sales by a big percentage since last year. 36% more or something like that.
Arthur:	They were saying that last month was the best month they'd ever had in the factory. But they're even making some up in Liverpool.
Spen:	Are they?
Arthur:	They're making them at Haywood, the old Jaguar place. I don't know whether the Jaguar is still made there.
Michael:	I think they make some small Jags there.
Arthur:	They made the small Jags. That's still a runner.
Alex:	I don't know. I think it might be being replaced.
Arthur:	You don't see a lot of the small Jags about anymore, but maybe you will in future.
Spen:	They lost out. There's one that's really a Ford underneath isn't it?
Arthur:	Oh, I think on a Mondeo.
Spen:	Yes, which is perfectly alright. But I think they made it look wrong. You know, the styling is enormously important.
Arthur:	No. They had to make it four wheel drive because the torque of the engine was a bit too high for the back axle.
Spen:	Well whether it was that. I think there was the catch. They didn't want it to be called a front wheel drive car, that's what it was.
Arthur:	Oh that's what it was. I see. (laughs)
Spen:	So I don't think it was engineering. I think it was just it didn't look right. Now they're making it from aluminium you know

Arthur:	I wouldn't look at the whole car. You've got the whole body in white. Is it the same fancy alloy that we were using, that Birmabright 3% magnesium stuff? Or is it invented new ones now?
Spen:	It's something like that. It's a special alloy to suit the job. And it's probably a magnesium aluminium. I don't know.
Arthur:	Remember Robert Boyle? Did Robert Boyle have his boat made out of the same materials, *The Four Freedoms?*
Spen:	Yes, *The Four Freedoms*, that's right. I remember when *The Four Freedoms* got hit by a trawler in the side.
Arthur:	That's right. He was reviewing the fleet at the time. (laughs) He wasn't looking where he was going or the trawler wasn't. I'm not sure which. (laughs) Anyway the trawler won. There was no argument about that.
Spen:	It still beat aluminium then.
Arthur:	And the boat was actually bent, if you ran a line from the front to the centre to the back. It wasn't through the middle of the cab. It was dipped to one side. But that's unless you've got a circular run that you do, it wouldn't match up.
Spen:	It's like this all the time. It didn't leak, though I think when it got hit like that, it didn't sink.
Arthur:	The first thing. The first time we took it out, it made a big dent at the front. It was slamming pretty badly. And it pushed the front up between the stiffeners. When they designed the stiffeners, I think they thought the material was a bit stiffer than it turned out to be. But that material used to work hardened. We used to run half hard and quarter hard and bring it up by the process. I think on this dent in, it hadn't hardened itself. And it was still soft but by the time it got bent right up the wrong way. Then, of course, it was hard. (laughs)
Spen:	That's right. And it didn't wanna go back again.
Arthur:	(laughs)
Spen:	Poor old Robert. He had some grief with that boat I think.
Arthur:	Oh he did, yeah. He also invented an airgun you know.

Michael Bishop

Arthur's Factory Tour at Land Rover in 2010.

Spen:	Yes, I know. A pump up airgun.
Arthur :	I thought he'd have shot himself with it at times with that boat. Yes, it was a good idea. It didn't have big heavy parts crashing and banging about while he was trying to hold it still.
Spen:	What? The airgun?
Arthur :	Mmmm.
Spen:	Yes. Of course, Maurice was an air pistol shooter.
Arthur :	Was he?
Spen:	Yes. I think he was quite good at it actually. And he designed his own air pistols I think as well. There was a pair. You know they were friends really doing the air pistols
Arthur :	I bet they'd have had some fun with that. Yes, he sort of pumped the thing up. And then just released the gas or the air. If you like, instead of having a big thing with the spring and a piston that goes crunch. (laughs)
Spen:	Yeah. I think they're pretty lethal weapons actually. They've got quite a high muzzle velocity.
Arthur :	Muzzle velocity though is approaching one of the shorter two two's, (.22 calibre) not the long cartridge ones.
Spen:	Two thousand feet per second.
Arthur :	That's right. Of course it didn't weigh very much. That would be his next job, making it a twelve bore.
Spen:	It's best not to get shot, just the same.
Arthur :	Yeah. So there we go. So I've had an exciting week, and I've got an exciting week coming up
Spen:	When are you going back?
Arthur :	And then I shall disappear back to work. (talking to Alex) Have your dad after me again. His dad's got a factory opposite ours.
Spen:	What does that do?
Arthur :	He makes coffins.
Spen:	Stockings?

Arthur :	Coffins, dozens of them. They've got a production line for these. And he keeps coming over and asking me how I am you see. And he got this tape measure out and (inaudible) me off a little bit. And then he offers me a special deal, because he's got one and they've made it too big or too small or something. And I can have it cheap and he'll keep it til I'm ready, you know. So he's a good lad but that's where all this Land Rover business started, your Land Rover I think I can't remember now. Yours (at Alex) that started it. And Chris said "have a word with Arthur, he used to work on those things." But people think I really worked on them myself, you know. Well I didn't really dirty my hands that much on it. (laughs) I used to put a white coat on and make it look as though I did.
Spen:	Oh. I remember you in a white. You wore a white coat. Yes. That's right. But you had a problem with shimmy on the (Land Rover) front axle, didn't you?
Arthur :	Oh, very much so. Yes.
Spen:	And did you end up by putting the shackles at the other end of the springs?
Arthur :	We certainly did. We cured it. We disguised it by putting damping in the system. And that was quite tricky, because the damping had to really only effect one end so it didn't put up the steering effort significantly, but offered a lot of resistance at the bottom.
Spen:	Frictional damping is a horrible thing in steering, actually.
Arthur :	Well, what we did. The front wheel drive. The casing of the front wheel drive was really top and bottom for the Kingpin. Only they hadn't got the Kingpin. And it had Timkin taper roller bearings well on the one taking the load, which is the top one. I took out the centre of the Timkin bearing and made one out of Tufnol and put that in and that stopped it. It worked very well, and you could hardly feel it from the top end.
Spen:	It depends on your standard of judgement, actually. For the Land Rover, it sounded as if it was ok. (laughter)

Arthur :	I was biased. (laughs) Passed with flying colours. (laughs)
Arthur :	And then we put the springs the other way around and that fixed it. The only thing we'd ever do is ever figure out why (laughs) we just accepted that as a gift and got on.
Spen:	With a positive energy input, it goes worse and worse. If it's dampened it doesn't.
Arthur :	There's all sorts of fancy ideas and theories and things like that.
Spen:	Yeah, there was a lot of theories around.
Arthur :	And centres of procession. Somebody invented centres of procession. It was you, wasn't it?
Spen:	It's not me, I heard about them, but I didn't invent them.
Arthur:	I thought god, what's that? (laughs) When they say "this is where you hit it with a cricket bat and you don't feel anything."
Spen:	That's right.
Arthur :	Yeah. Well that's a great help.
Spen:	If the ball hits the bat at the very bottom or the top it stings your hand. (laughs)
Michael:	I've always wondered about that.
Spen:	What? About centres of procession?
Michael:	Yeah. Cricket bats because I was so short sighted as a kid. I had my eyes lasered and fixed. And I got a lot better as I was older, but I used to always try (to play) but I couldn't. Because I was so short sighted, with a good fast bowler I couldn't see the ball. So I hoped I just get that sweet spot.
Spen:	Well I used to try and play cricket. That was my joke to have ball fly past you.
Arthur :	I remember watching you play cricket and for the life of me I was thinking where it could have been.

Spen:	I was a bowler.
Arthur :	Where were you playing cricket?
Spen:	We used to do it inside Rover company cricket matches between the gas turbine department.
Arthur :	That's what it was.
Spen:	I can remember Gallaford. Do you remember him?
Arthur :	Oh, yes.
Spen:	Being a big fat batsman, and I was a bowler. And I got him in the middle of his stomach. (laughs)
Arthur :	Yes. I remember.
Spen:	That was a long time ago. I wouldn't do things like that anymore. (All laugh.)
Arthur :	That was the biggest target he had.
Spen:	It was a super target, yes. Tom Barton, you remember, do you?
Arthur :	Yes.
Spen:	He came through. It was really the moving spirit of Land Rover.
Arthur :	Yes. He was in the end.
Spen:	He got to the customer, you know, particularly military customers. And found out what they didn't like and what they did like and all that sort of thing. And actually got it to happen inside the company
Arthur :	They've slipped a bit on the military side now from what it used to be.
Spen:	I think they have, yes.
Arthur :	That could do with a good kick in the pants.
Spen:	Well, I think the trouble is that they didn't. You know the demand things which are very special, wouldn't fit in sort of thing to the Land Rover scheme of doing things. Because, if you remember, there was an Austin Champ and another vehicle which was even more special and funny. And they were exactly what the military wanted but they cost so bloody much, they couldn't afford them. That's why the Land Rover got into the military.

Arthur :	You're absolutely right. And of course, we'd done all the simple things. They stored the shovel and the Jerry can and a few things for them, but we didn't change the basics.
Spen:	That was the whole idea of the thing, not to change the basics as the same as a civil vehicle.
Arthur :	But we couldn't. If we changed the basics, Poppe would have died.
Spen:	What?
Arthur :	Poppe would have died if you'd have changed the basics on the Land Rover.
Spen:	Yes, but if you now said "Oh I know, I'll make Land Rover to sell to the military" and went to the military and find out what they want, you'd have to change the whole damn Land Rover to satisfy them I think.
Arthur :	Yes, it's a pity that.
Arthur:	Well, we better make a move I think.
Michael:	No problem.
Arthur :	Otherwise I might be thrown out of my lodgings. (laughs)

The post Rover years onwards

To find out the circumstances in how Arthur seemed to disappear where he went with Girling was of great importance to us Land Rover enthusiasts. From a general car fan point of view very interesting as well. Arthur's career move to automotive brake manufacturer Girling was a fantastic opportunity for him. No doubt his success at Rover got him the job. Girling offered Arthur a fantastic package. He got the top engineering job of Technical Director as well as position on the Lucas Girling Board. The job was to the level that he was very eager to achieve at this stage of his career. The move to Girling was also huge change. Technical Director at Girling Brakes was the top of the tree for that side of the Lucas Girling business and had a very broad scope. Girling supplied brake components to many of the worlds leading manufacturers. For Arthur who was never too worried about the pretty parts of a car it was a perfect match and na area that would demand his undivided attention on innovative ideas to stay at leading edge of braking engineering and development. Girlings structure and decision making was quite different to that of Rover. Arthur admits at first he would have happily gone back to Rover, where he had so much freedom from having worked his way up the ladder. In addition, as a consequence of Arthur becoming a director at Lucas/Girling, his elder brother Les, who already worked for the Lucas Aerospace division, had to apply for an exception to retain his own job. This was because Lucas/Girling had a rule that board directors and any of their family members could not be employed by Lucas/Girling at the same time.

They Found Our Engineer

Arthur watches a Land Rover welder at use at the Nato Display at Rover's factory in early 1957 before he moved to Girling

Arthur's younger son, Chris and I feel there would be enough material in Arthur's career at Girling to write a book about this side of his career. Brakes, however; have never been thought of as glamorous part of a car. Also with such a broad scope where do you start your research? Arthur worked with so many great names and great companies where do you start? Alex and Russell took Arthur and Chris along to the Brisbane all British Day very early on into his reappearance to show Arthur the enthusiasm for older vehicles, restorations, old Rovers cars and Land Rovers. Alex recorded it on his video camera as well. After three hours of Arthur talking about car designs he liked and didn't like etc we still didn't know how to start. He had worked with almost everyone in the late 1950's and throughout the 1960's. But this also covered such a vast number of areas. Small cars, Luxury cars, Racing teams, different manufacturers and different countries were all part of the mix. With so many interlinking aspects to this stage of engineering Arthur's career, finding the whole story would be a challenge as well.

To get a snap shot of what he got up to in his job at Girling we found that Arthur was just as quick with an amusing story on the many areas and places where he worked. In talking away about these times, what did come out from Arthur were the entertaining tales that are just as fun to hear as the times they often had on the early Land Rover project. Many of these stories were on similar vein and as Arthur has often said with engineering almost everything is already known and just needs putting into context of the next idea. On the fun side, where elder son Stewart had Land Rover fire engines and Rover's Jet 1 Gas Turbine car brought home when he was a lad with Dad working a Rover. Younger Chris had a Ford GT40 brought home for him to 'play with' and trips to Italy and the Maserati factory where Arthur's good friend Gulio Alferi was Chief engineer. At Girling Arthur got to know quite a few people in motorsport given his position and the work was always fascinating, being it the Rover BRM Le Man winning Gas Turbine car or supplying brake components to F1 teams. Amusing situations he found as well. Enzo Ferrari refused to use Girling brakes as they were on Maseratis cars. Arthur says though Enzo was a clever chap and many items good and innovative in the motoring world, would end up with a 'Ferrari' version on Enzos cars.

Girling had many successes during Arthur's leadership. To touch on just a couple they managed to get their products onto European cars through supplying their disc brakes to manufacturers on the continent. Girling had managed to leap into the Disc brake market that was initially tightly held by Dunlop who had introduced modern disc brakes to the mainstream market in the 1950's. Arthur says the Dunlop disc brake pads and lining material were also part of the location tab that aligned the pad. This meant that they had the tendency to stick at times as the cylinders compressed the pads. So Arthur made sure the Girling location tab was just part of the metal base plate of the pad, and the pad itself was always to be smaller than the base plate to avoid this issue and his didn't stick. This simple innovation saw Girling get the jump on Dunlop's discs. Mercedes Benz was one of the first European manufacturers to use Girling Disc brakes on their 1961 220E. As well like some of Arthur's military testing stories on the Land Rovers, where they ended up in tricky situations. He has similar ones with his Girling career. Such as when component factories for Mercedes at this time had to be in Germany but weren't as well as other amusing boarder crossing stories to try and sort out such issues that were part of the time in those days.

One of Arthur's memorable and amusing stories during his visit was one of going to see Alec Issigonis and his new Mini in the late 50's at prototype stage. Arthur was meeting with Alec about the braking needs for the car. He had become good friends with Alec too. Both had worked under Robert Boyle at different stages in their careers. We know Arthur always said marketing and knowing what would sell were something he never really had a feel for and this was no different for Alec's Mini. Arthur couldn't believe it how small the original Mini was and infamously put his foot in it. He said he thought it would never sell and happily admits it too. The Mini was part of the British Motor Corporation at this early stage and part of the badge engineering stage as the vehicle was released as the Austin 7 and the Morris Mini Minor and obviously went onto being a huge success.

Arthurs time as Girling Technical Director also lead to a number of patents that are in Arthur and Girling's name. It also took him into doing lectures to engineers on braking efficiency and developments in the industry. Some Russian engineers were in one of Arthur's lectures and approached him after to do some work with them on one of their cars, in the Communist state. Arthur had no issues with this and this lead to a problem that was found on the Russian Presidential Cars made by ZIL or Zavod imeni Likhachova in Russia. It was a vast heavy thing. A very 60's looking limousine with an equally huge V8 engine. The weight had got the better of the brakes efficiency on the ZIL. So Arthur got the job of going to Moscow in around 1970 and sorting it out. This was height of the iron curtain and the cold war between Russia and the US and its Allies. Arthurs visit was a kept very quiet and even though he and his colleague were lent one of these vast beasts, they were put in a hotel at night and told not to leave and travel too far or else. They were though given huge bunch of raffle tickets type coupons that they couldn't read. Western money was completely useless, but they soon figured out these tickets were coupons for food, wine, and vodka at the Restaurant over the road. So they just ordered everything they could and just kept handing over the book of tickets to the waiter and let him take what he needed and lived like Kings. Having the Presidential car too they realised that each post they went past the guards, police and all sundry all stood and saluted, so they soon started exploring the greater area to see what was about. They realised they would never be stopped and questioned given the car they had. They thought it was a great laugh. The brakes on the cars got sorted out to and redesigned to be much better for the weight they were using. It was at this time that Arthur was contacted and asked to head out to Australia to be Managing Director of Automotive and Girling. A joint venture company that made Girlock brakes for the Australian motor industry.

Arthur disappears to Sydney.

Arthur was told that Automotive and Girling in Australia wasn't running so well, so Arthur's job was to get it back on track. The Australian Motor industry was and still is basically lead by Ford, General Motors-Holden. In those days Chrysler as to, but also with CKD and part KD plants for many other manufacturers who they also supplied. After a few years of restructuring and cost cutting, Automotive and Girling started to turn around and Arthur was enjoying Australia. He found he had a lot more opportunity to play Golf in his past time. Younger son Chris had come with him out to Sydney and went to school there and they had a great place to live in near the Harbour. It was a great lifestyle to have but by the mid 1970's Arthur was looking forward to retiring and moving back to England. One interesting event in his time in Australia did appear. It was the Inquiry by the Federal Government into road safety. The brakes on many Australian made cars had come into question and the House of Representatives Standing Committee on Road Safety was looking for answers and called on international braking expert, Mr Arthur Goddard to report his findings.

The Age Newspaper 19 June 1975,
Braking on Australian Cars Worst : Expert
SYDNEY - *A comparison of the brakes on Australian, European and American Cars showed that Australian brakes are worst, according to evidence before a Government committee on road safety.*

An international car brake expert showed that the average Australian car brakes have half the capacity of European brakes to dissipate heat and resist fading, under hard driving conditions.

They Found Our Engineer

Australian cars also had 10 per cent less braking capacity than U.S. models said, Mr. Arthur Goddard, managing director of Automotive and Girling.

He told the House of Representatives standing committee on road safety that in comparative braking results, Australia's high power sedans produced the worst results with the Valiant Charger E49 scoring only 2.1 points compared with the Australian average of 3.3.

On the international table the Peugeot 504 scored highest of all with 10 points.

The average European car scored 7 and the average U.S. score was 3.6.

The (Holden) Torana SL/R scored 2.3 points, the (Ford) Fairlane 351 2.5 points and the (Holden) Monaro GTS 2.6.

The (Holden) Torana 2850 with 4.8, scored the best braking of Australian cars, followed by the Holden 202, 4.7 and the (Ford) Falcon 250, 4.2.

Mr. Goddard to the committee that Automotive and Girling designed and manufactured brakes for leading international car companies and also made brakes for local manufacturers, Ford, GM-H and Chrysler.

In recent years Girling, in conjunction with its parent company, Joseph Lucas industries had developed a sophisticated anti skid braking system called electronic wheel skid protection (WSP)

WSP was a 'black box' device which would enable a drive to maintain steering control of a vehicle under all conditions.

Mr. Goddard said WSP could be fitted to passenger vehicles for $100.

He said however that the black box raised philosophical and legal problems because it took control away from the driver.

Mr. Goddard said that a combination of four wheel disc brakes and a special pressure control valve could be fitted to production cars for about $20 to improve safety.

Having grown up in Australia, surrounded by the huge following of these iconic Australian Muscle Cars, in finding this made me really laugh out loud. As amongst the awe and passion behind these cars is a huge element of the typical Aussie, 'She'll be right mate' belief and possibly in the braking systems of these cars as well. The issue made the front page of the national paper *The Australian* on the same day and wasn't the end of it. Arthur wasn't too popular.

The story was followed up a few days later with Ford Australia clearly defending the brake designs on their cars and the Government committee wanting and waiting to 'hear more from the manufactures' before finalising their report.

Arthur with Taz Katsamas's superbly restored 1950 80" Land Rover

While Arthur and I were driving up from Heathrow on his visit to England and Land Rover, we were discussing all things Rover and Girling. So I threw the Parliamentary Inquiry into the conversation. Arthur laughed. 'You found out that too?' So what transpired is that concern was raised about the braking efficiency in these cars and the fade as well. Some problems had occurred, hence why there was a Government inquiry and Arthur was called as the expert on automotive brakes.

Australians love of 6 cylinders engines and large capacity V8's in their cars was at it height in the early 70's and competition between these three manufacturers was not only in the market place but on the race track too. The Holden vs Ford saga at the Bathurst 1000 was just as big then as it is now in Australian racing. The Aussie car enthusiasts catch phrase was, 'There is no replacement for displacement', which means for the best performance get one with a V8 in it.

The problem however was that the platforms of these cars came from the parent companies either in the US or Europe of each of them. The designs had minimum specifications for the vehicle to operate safely. They could be engineered to take the huge engines, but the brakes were at times somewhat overlooked to an extent.

So the Holden Torana which in the UK and Europe is an Opel Ascona, that came with a 1.9 litre 4 cylinder. But in Oz it came not only with the 1.9 litre engine but also 2.8 and 3.3 litre sixes for the 'family car' as well as 4.2 and 5.0 litre V8's for the 'boy racers'. The issues are plainly obvious if the brakes weren't upgraded at quite the same rate as the engines the cars simply wouldn't stop.

Arthur said all this caused one hell of a storm but he wasn't going to say anything other than what he could see of the situation. Shortly after he visited the Detroit Motor show and Ford's top brass there thanked Arthur for bringing the brake issues to the surface for their cars in Australia as they weren't aware of the issue at all and no doubt caused all involved a few sleepless nights at the time.

No doubt at this point as people in England were starting to delve into Land Rover's history 1970's Australia was a long way from home. Communication across the world was mostly still letters and was for a long time to come. So Arthur just slipped below the enthusiasts radar for years to come.

The post retirement Career

Arthur along with his current research & development off road trailer and Alex's 1948 Land Rover

At the end of the 1970's Arthur retired. He had a stellar engineering career and and a leaving party in Australia and England. He moved back to England, to the Midlands not far from Solihull and bought himself a Porsche. He had never had to have his own car so bought something flash and that the golf clubs could fit in it. But after 6 months he was bored. He got a new offer from back in Australia. This time Quiton Hazzel Motor parts needed restructuring with warehouses in Sydney and Melbourne and they had got in touch, as he had done such a great job with Girling. He was back in Oz in a flash and stayed with them to the mid 1980's. To make sure he didn't get bored again Arthur bought himself a project. A trailer axle manufacturing business, called Vehicle Components, in Brisbane. After leaving Quinton Hazell he moved up to Brisbane and started running Vehicle Components himself that mostly supplied caravan axles.

Arthur found that more and more people were travelling in caravans and getting right off the beaten track and into the outback and off road with their vans. So he started to look at the off road options to make things smoother and stronger for Caravan use. When he got to the point of employing over 20 staff he had son Chris come and run it for him, so he could step back and work on the areas he liked where he is still Chief Engineer. Chris after school in Sydney had moved back to study engineering in England and got a job at Girling. He met some of Arthur's old colleagues and worked with them, including Johnny Cullen who was at Girling as well in the late 70's and early 80's before he retired. Chris went onto work for many of Land Rover's suppliers in the 80's and early 1990's and was happy to move to Brisbane with his young family when Dad called for him to come and help run the business in Brisbane.

It was when they outgrew their first factory that Chris started looking for another and made the fateful move to opposite Russell Massey's business. Brisbane is a city of just over 2 million people, of which the Land Rover Register and Series One club combined may have up to a dozen past and present members their who may have been able to 'find' Arthur if they had come across him. So the odds of finding him were very low. That move by Vehicle Components of their factory for everyone who has enjoyed this story was the one amazing piece of good fortune and with out it none of this find of Arthur Goddard would have happened. Stewart, Chris and his greater family had wanted to get Arthur's Land Rover story going a bit and tell it somehow. However they didn't quite no how to go about it. But, as I said at the start, history usually somehow bubbles away and finally 'floats to the surface'.

When I visited Vehicle Components in October 2010 to talk Land Rovers, Arthur was in the throws of completing some new improvements to one of their core products, his off road trailer hitch. It works a touch like a universal joint and moves in all directions needed allowing the trailer incredible movement and stability off road. But it is also way stronger than a simple universal joint hitch. We all had a great chat about what had happened recently and what else is still being found on his days at Rover. Always looking forward Arthur mentioned what else he was doing. His bad knee he had when he arrived to visit England had finally come good so he was back on the golf course and no doubt he had a ball running around back at Land Rover in Solihull earlier in the year. They had a heap more products and innovations happening at Vehicle Components that Arthur needed to help stay in front of the game and his factory was buzzing with activity. He would be back in a flash to visit England again if he could get the time!

Printed in Great Britain
by Amazon